PRAISE FOR
A Broken Hallelujah

"This is a wise book, and it asks poignant and ⌐ ⌐s-
tions. . . . Now, as Cohen continues to create powe ⌐me-
less music, the time is right for an elegant examination of the
man's work: his passions, his fears, his poetry, his anger, his
loneliness, his redemption. The time is right for Leibovitz's
A Broken Hallelujah." —Alan W. Petrucelli, *Examiner*

"Less about Suzanne than 'Suzanne,' Leibovitz's book high-
lights the novelist behind the songwriter, the poet behind the
novelist, and the would-be prophet looming over them all."
—Marc Dolan, author of
Bruce Springsteen and the Promise of Rock 'n' Roll

"As I sat down to read *A Broken Hallelujah*, I couldn't help
but wonder if I'd find it to be no more than a rehashing of
already published material. I'm delighted to report that this
thought-provoking book not only stands on its own, it is absolutely outstanding." —Naomi Tropp, *Jewish Book World*

"Amusing and thoughtful." —BookReporter.com

"I am grateful for Liel Leibovitz's thoughtful attempt to divine
the motivations of this thoroughly original soul. *A Broken
Hallelujah*, in its best moments, represents a new approach
to the art of biography." —Robert Dean Lurie,
Front Porch Republic

"A warm, lovely invitation to appreciate Cohen's art and influences." —*Midwest Book Review*

"This book is for both those looking for something in addition to what the biographies tell and those less interested in the facts than in just thinking about the songs." —Tom Gallagher, *San Francisco Chronicle*

"Leibovitz shines a light on Jewish eschatology, Zen Buddhism, Canadian poetry, and the rigors of wanderlust and melancholia." —Frederic and Mary Ann Brussat, *Spirituality and Practice*

A Broken Hallelujah

*Fortunate Sons: The 120 Chinese Boys Who Came
to America, Went to School, and Revolutionized an
Ancient Civilization* (with Matthew Miller)

*The Chosen Peoples: America, Israel, and the Ordeals
of Divine Election* (with Todd Gitlin)

Lili Marlene: The Soldiers' Song of World War II
(with Matthew Miller)

*Aliya: Three Generations of American-Jewish
Immigration to Israel*

A Broken Hallelujah

Rock and Roll, Redemption,
and the Life of
Leonard Cohen

LIEL LEIBOVITZ

W. W. Norton & Company
New York • London

Since this page cannot legibly accommodate all
the copyright notices, pages 247–49 constitute an
extension of the copyright page.

For information about permission to reproduce
selections from this book, write to Permissions,
W. W. Norton & Company, Inc.,
500 Fifth Avenue, New York, NY 10110

For information about special discounts for
bulk purchases, please contact W. W. Norton
Special Sales at specialsales@wwnorton.com
or 800-233-4830

Manufacturing by RR Donnelley, Harrisonburg
Book design by Lisa Buckley Design
Production manager: Devon Zahn

Library of Congress Cataloging-in-Publication Data

Leibovitz, Liel.
   A broken hallelujah : rock and roll, redemption, and
the life of Leonard Cohen / Liel Leibovitz.
      pages cm
   Includes bibliographical references and index.
   ISBN 978-0-393-08205-0 (hardcover)
   1. Cohen, Leonard, 1934– 2. Composers—Canada—
Biography. 3. Singers—Canada—Biography. I. Title.
   ML410.C734L45 2014
   782.42164092—dc23
   [B]
                        2013047874

ISBN 978-0-393-35073-9 pbk.

W. W. Norton & Company, Inc.
500 Fifth Avenue, New York, N.Y. 10110
www.wwnorton.com

W. W. Norton & Company Ltd.
Castle House, 75/76 Wells Street, London W1T 3QT

1 2 3 4 5 6 7 8 9 0

To Lisa and Lily,
whose love is the engine of my survival

Contents

A Broken Hallelujah

Preface

This is not a biography of Leonard Cohen. Leonard Cohen himself already delivered the best possible account of his life, in a letter to the Canadian Broadcasting Corporation, written when he was twenty-nine. Here it is, in its entirety: "I was born in Montreal, September 21, 1934. My passport number is 5-017560. My eyes are hazel."[1] He was writing to enter his most recent collection of poems, *Flowers for Hitler*, in a contest for young writers. He might have been better served had he mentioned his previous two books of poetry, both well received, or his modest fame, or earlier prizes he had won. He didn't. The thing being judged was his work, and whatever morsel of his personal life he felt comfortable enough sharing with strangers would find its way, after a process of mild sublimation, into a book. Or an album: Years later, as a celebrated musician, he remained reluctant to divulge too much. In interviews he'd reply that the only answers that mattered were there in his songs.

To look for clues elsewhere, in lists of accomplishments or in the particulars of love affairs or in the knots of familial entanglements, is to assume that an artist's work is just a stage on which some larger drama is being performed. It is to believe that there's a Rosebud, some critical moment that explains everything and that enough digging can reveal. And it is not a very gratifying approach, particularly when the subject at hand is a singer and a poet whose words, like the chants of Gregorian monks, seem designed to attract the attention of some higher power. What more might we learn about "So Long, Marianne," for example, by knowing that the woman who inspired the song met Leonard Cohen in the agora of the Greek island of Hydra, or that she was walking with her blond husband and blond baby and looked, to a lonely Cohen, like the holy ghost of a beautiful, tanned trinity?[2] The song leaves us with difficult ideas, like what it means to be almost young or what happens when the angels forget to pray for us. The story, on the other hand, is just gossamer—airy gossip that fades away with time.

Once people knew I was writing a book about him, I heard a lot of stories about Leonard Cohen. I spoke to some of his friends and fellow musicians, scoured his letters and notebooks, and read my way through five decades of press interviews. None of these helped explain his strange career. Cohen, as the journalist Bruce Headlam noted, belongs to an exclusive club of entertainers—Ray Charles may be the only other member—who don't really fit into any one particular era, always at odds with the times: "He was too young to be a Beat, too old to be a folkie, and he announced he wanted to change the face of Canadian literature before there really was one. He lived in Tennessee near Nashville in the early 1970s, before the country-music revival, and in the 1980s, when everybody went super-chroma, he stayed black and white. By the early 1990s, when everyone else was depressed, Cohen—the Dr. Kevorkian of pop music—began to have fun, cutting music videos, graciously accepting awards . . . and appearing at Hollywood functions with his girl friend, actress Rebecca De Mornay."[3] His twelfth studio album, *Old Ideas*, released in 2012 when he was seventy-seven years old, was his first to make it into the Billboard top ten chart; the rest had barely registered. Adored in Europe, he was such an anomaly to U.S. audiences that in 1984, Walter Yetnikoff, the monarch of Columbia Records, summoned Cohen to a meeting, looked at the middle-aged singer's dark double-breasted suit, and said, "Look, Leonard, we know you're great, but we don't know if you're any good." It was Yetnikoff's way of telling Cohen that the label had decided not to distribute his latest album, *Various Positions*, in the United States. It wasn't, Yetnikoff said, contemporary enough.[4] The culture eventually caught up with Cohen: The album's centerpiece, an anthem about love and redemption dense with biblical imagery, became one of the most frequently covered songs of the last three decades. In 2008, for example, no fewer than three versions of "Hallelujah" scaled Britain's Top 50 chart,[5] and the song graced the sound tracks of blockbuster movies, from *Shrek* to *The Watchmen*.

Little about Cohen's life illuminates these wild oscillations. His story fits snugly into what can be called rock and roll's ur-biography: He lost a parent at an early age (like John Lennon, Paul McCartney, Jimi Hendrix, Neil Young), found comfort in poetry (like Jim Morrison, Joni Mitchell, Patti Smith), left his native country and settled somewhere exotic for a spell (Morrison again, Keith Richards), did mounds of drugs (pretty much everyone), wrestled with depression (David Bowie, Syd Barrett, Brian Wilson), and lived long enough to see himself becoming an icon to younger musicians (the few, the fortunate). But most of Leonard Cohen's peers are either four decades dead or ambling onto stages in never-ending nostalgia concert tours, and he's becoming better somehow, or at least more culturally salient and more commercially popular. We smile when Mick Jagger takes the stage and attempts all the old Stones classics, because we understand that there's something amusing about a man his age trying to recapture the same libidinal thrusts that made him so sexy and cool nearly half a century ago. But when Leonard Cohen, a decade Jagger's senior, walks up to the microphone, nobody laughs. You feel the same hum at a Cohen concert that you do in a church or a synagogue, a feeling that emanates from the realization that the words and the tunes you're about to hear represent the best efforts we humans can make to capture the mysteries that surround us, and that by listening and closing your eyes and singing along, you, too, can somehow transcend. We have better poets than Leonard Cohen, and more skilled novelists. Songwriters blessed with greater talent wrote songs and gained fame and withered away. But Leonard Cohen lingers and thrives because he is not really any of these things, at least not essentially. He's something more intricate, the sort of man whose pores absorb the particles of beauty and grief and truth that float weightlessly all around us yet so few of us note. He is attuned to the divine, whatever the divine might be, not with the thinker's complications or the zealot's obstructions, but with the unburdened heart of a believer—it's not for nothing that he referred to himself in song as "the little Jew who wrote the Bible." Millennia ago, as we began asking ourselves the same fundamental questions we still ponder, we called men like him prophets, meaning not that they could foresee the future but that they could better understand the present by seeing one more layer of meaning to life. The title still applies.

So what is the prophet Cohen telling us? And why do we listen so intently? These are the questions at the heart of this book. They're not easy ones to answer: Some themes, like theology or rock and roll or orgasms, often wilt when captured between the covers of a book, and Leonard Cohen's body of work is obsessed with all three in more or less equal measure. To study them without robbing them of their vitality, we need to observe them in their natural environment. Sometimes they are best understood when considered through a particular story from Cohen's life; at others they require more remote meditations. They cut across the fields of Jewish eschatology and Zen Buddhism, Canadian poetry and American rock and roll, lust and lucre. They're not always accessible to reason. But they've given us our man, and with him the license to reconsider the sort of sentiments—grace, redemption—that, until late in our adolescence as a species, took up most of our time and that now, when we're all mature, sound too wild to be relevant and too dangerous to roam outside some intellectual discipline's cage. And the only appropriate thing for us to say in return is Hallelujah.

Prelude

The rusty green jeep could barely make it up the hill, so Mick Farren climbed out, put his hand to his forehead to shade his eyes from the glare of the late August sun, and surveyed the island.[1] He'd never been to the Isle of Wight before, and little about it interested him now. Had he turned around and looked to the north, he would have seen a sliver of the island's spectacular shoreline, which, with its salt-stricken limestone cliffs, looked like the footprint of some enormous animal long extinct. But Farren was looking south, staring downhill at two snaking lines of corrugated metal fencing in a large patch of grass patrolled by men in navy blue uniforms and German shepherds in tight leather collars. Farren shook his head. The whole scene, he told his driver, reminded him of East Germany or, worse, of Dachau. He pointed at the large stage erected at the heart of the encampment, a rickety-looking thing with the words "music festival" painted on a scaffold in bright, cheerful colors. The festival, he said to no one in particular, had to be freed.

A few days later, Farren received a phone call from the festival's producer, Rikki Farr.[2] Their similar-sounding names weren't the only points of resemblance between the two men: They were both in their twenties, both the sons of working-class English families, born shortly after the Second World War and set loose in their adolescence by the thrills and tumults of the 1960s. But whereas Rikki had long, straight blond hair and took an interest in managing musical acts that sang softly about love and peace, Mick wore his curly black hair like a mushroom cloud and fronted a band called the Deviants whose biggest hit was "Let's Loot the Supermarket." When they first met, sometime around 1966 or 1967, Farr and Farren could still talk genially about politics and music and the many people they knew in common in London's underground cultural scene. By 1970, however, Mick had formed a militia of pranksters he called the White Panthers, and had gained notoriety for such brazen acts as taking over a segment of David Frost's television show and shouting anarchist slogans. Farr had heard that Farren and his White Panthers were planning to show up at the Isle of Wight and pull off all sorts of riots. The last thing he needed to contend with just a day before the festival was scheduled to begin were troublemakers like Mick Farren.

The producer, Farren later recalled, said something about peace and love and good vibes. Farren had little patience for such slogans, and accused Farr of having no other motive but money. Defending himself, Farr replied that given the festival's stellar lineup—he had booked the Doors, Hendrix, the Who, Joni Mitchell, and virtually every other major musical act of the time—there was little else he could do but charge for admission. The artists had to be paid, he calmly explained, as did the carpenters who built the stage, the electricians and the roadies and everyone else needed to put together a five-day-long festival. Farren mumbled something about music wanting to be free, but Farr could take it no longer. He hung up.

As the first swarms of concertgoers stepped off the ferry on Wednesday, August 26, 1970, there was little to suggest that Farren's threats might come to fruition. The youth who'd arrived looked like decent kids. They had long hair and big smiles, and many of them lived off unemployment payments doled out by the British government. They bought their tickets for three pounds sterling and rushed into the festival's fenced-in area to catch a good spot on the grass in front of the stage. They swayed dreamily to the progressive rock band Judas Jump, and cheered warmly for the California folksinger Kathy Smith and her two-hour-long set of mellow tunes. A clean-shaven Kris Kristofferson was there, too, but the sound system stuttered, and his set was soon inaudible. The crowd was kind, protesting mildly, clapping when appropriate. Rikki Farr apologized profusely, promising Kristofferson he could play a second set in a day or two. Despite all the technical glitches, Farr was certain that the event he'd worked for more than a year to make real was going to be epic. It would be, he told his friends at the tent he set up as the production's makeshift office, England's Woodstock.

On Thursday morning, with seventy thousand ticketholders already in attendance, Farr pranced onto the stage to introduce Supertramp, an unknown band a few weeks away from releasing its first album. "I can see we're going to have one hell of a great festival!" he said. "You got your rocks off, right? You know, I think I'm going to come down there and join you, because that's obviously the place to be at the moment."

But Farr spent most of his time in the production tent backstage, where cash was quickly piling up. He needn't have been much of an experienced promoter to realize, a day after its inauguration, that the Isle of Wight festival was slated to be massively profitable: The main attractions were still a day or two away from taking the stage, and if the current attendance rate was any indication, it stood to draw upward of two hundred thousand people. With the sort of satisfied smile reserved only for particularly auspicious problems, Farr asked a young assistant to get on the phone and inquire about procuring more portable toilets: The festival's rows of wooden commodes, he said, might not be enough.

Such problems, however, lay in the future. For the time being the patch of grass known as East Afton Farm looked as orderly and well maintained as a camping ground, with tents strewn at reasonable intervals from one another and communal bonfires bringing together strangers for shared impromptu meals. If Woodstock was strong American coffee, quipped one festivalgoer, then Wight was weak English tea, comforting but not particularly arousing. Two more days of mild music proved his point. Most of the artists taking the stage—Chicago, Procol Harum, and Rikki Farr's brother, Gary, an R & B crooner with sandy hair and a sweet voice—seemed like throwbacks to the mid-1960s, to the era before Dylan went electric and the Hells Angels went to Altamont and the promises of change curdled into violence or, worse, despair. Listening to the melodies floating through the farm, struggling sometimes to overcome the din of the waves crashing on the cliffs, one could think that whatever demons were clawing at America's social and political fabrics, they had not yet crossed the Atlantic.

And then came the weekend.

At first, sometime late Friday morning, someone tapped Rikki Farr on the shoulder and asked him who were all those people hanging out on the hill just above East Afton Farm. Probably nobodies, Farr said, probably just a bunch of kids who couldn't afford the ticket or were too stingy to pay. By the late afternoon, however, the crowd of stragglers grew thicker. Each arriving ferry seemed to unload more and more people headed not to the fenced-in festival site but up to the hill. By the time the sun had set and the Voices of East Harlem children's choir took the stage, the ticketholders inside the encampment were in the minority.

It didn't take much guessing to figure out who was behind the sudden influx of freeloaders. Furious, Farr grabbed the phone and again called Mick Farren. When he heard the anarchist's sleepy voice on the other end, Farr lost his temper. As Farren later recalled the conversation, the producer threatened to kill him. Their talk went nowhere.[3] Farr slammed the phone against his makeshift desk and ran outside to observe the situation.

What he saw was jarring. No longer content with merely watching the concert from their elevated vantage point, the mob on the hill tumbled toward the festival site, rolling against the metal fences and confronting the guards and their dogs. Mostly newcomers to keeping the peace, the guards wanted no trouble, nor did they know what to do if the hill people decided to attack. For every step the free-music crowd took forward, the guards took two back. Even if they had stood their ground, there still would have been little they could have done to keep the mob at bay—with the fence snaking on for nearly half a mile, all anyone needed to do to get in was stroll along the perimeter, find an unguarded spot, shake the thin leaves of metal until they bent, and crawl underneath. One by one, muddied men and women were spotted inside the festival's grounds, their hair just a little bit longer and their nudity just a little bit more pronounced. They were Mick Farren's minions, and Farr was determined to stop them.

From random conversations with a handful of the infiltrators, Rikki Farr learned that Farren had spread the word throughout London that the festival on Wight was being run by a cabal of greedy bastards, and that the thing to do was show up and demand that it be made free. A music journalist as well as an activist and a musician, Farren had written a series of articles in the underground press in the days leading up to the festival, urging his readers to take the first ferry out to the island. He had been there himself, he wrote, and had found just the spot from which to watch the concerts without pay; after "Desolation Row," Dylan's famous hymn of chaos and disillusion, he called it Desolation Hill.

The son of Tommy Farr, one of England's most renowned prizefighters, Rikki Farr grew up knowing all about tactics. Farren, it wasn't too difficult to realize, could only succeed if he managed to convince the masses that Farr and the festival's other organizers were money-hungry creeps bent on exploiting artists and audiences alike. The thing to do, Farr told his colleagues back in the production tent, was to show Farren's minions that the people who put the festival together were just a couple of like-minded cool cats: The thing to do was win them over.

Smiling broadly, Farr marched out to the field and headed straight for the fence. There, as he'd expected, were hundreds of the hill people, pushing against the fence and provoking the guards. Farr introduced himself. Immediately, the yelling began: *Pig! Let us in! Music is free!* Shouting to overcome the din of the crowd, Farr addressed a few dozen men who seemed to be the mob's most vociferous leaders, asking them to step aside and chat with him for a minute. When they did, he pulled out a crumpled wad of tickets and made them a simple offer. The fence, he said, was there only to guarantee everyone's safety, not to keep anyone out. That being the case, it should be painted in bright colors to reflect its true, peaceful mission. He promised the men free festival tickets if they collected a few of their friends, picked up some brushes, and redecorated the same sheets of metal they had spent the better part of the day trying to tear down. They accepted on the spot, and Farr dispatched an assistant to bring three hundred brushes and two hundred gallons of paint. He shook hands with each of his new hires and marched back to his tent, whistling happily. More bees with honey, he thought. It was going to be all right. Cactus, the American supergroup, gave a searing set, shredding the strings of their guitars, but Farr was exhausted. He collapsed on a cot in his tent and went to sleep.

He was awakened a few hours later by someone loudly shouting, "Fuckers!" Lazily Farr walked out to inspect. It was early in the morning. Most of the audience was sleeping. The hill people seemed to have ascended quietly to the top of their area. The festival grounds seemed as peaceful as they had been a few days prior, before hordes of barbarians knocked at its gates. But then a quick glance at the fence revealed everything. In bright colors, in big letters, slogans and symbols covered every inch of it: *Entrance is everywhere. Don't buy. Fuck the guards. Commune Free.* Farr's own name next to a swastika. The gambit that was designed to contain the troublemakers ended up giving them yards and yards of space to advertise their nonsense. Even worse, the artful vandals had all been given free tickets, and were now free to roam every corner of the grounds and dream up new mayhem.

Just what kind of mayhem they had in mind soon became evident. Joni Mitchell took the stage around noon and barely finished her third song when a shirtless gentleman leaped onstage, wrestled the microphone away from the stunned singer, introduced himself as Yogi Joe, and began his speech.

"Power to the people, motherfuckers!" he shouted. "I've been to Woodstock, and I dug it very much. I've been to about ten fucking festivals, and I love music. I just think one thing: this festival business is becoming a psychedelic concentration camp, where people are being exploited! And there's enough of that! What is all that peace and love shit when you have police dogs out there! What about that? That reminds me of a lot of bad things, you know? I don't like police dogs!"

He opened his mouth to say more, but Farr and Joni Mitchell's manager both jumped onstage and dragged him away. A roar of boos shook the air. A hundred bottles shot up like fireworks and made their way toward the stage. Mitchell looked stricken. "Listen a minute, will you?" she pleaded, sounding like a jilted lover begging for a second chance. "Will you listen a minute? Now listen! A lot of people who get up here and sing, I know it's fun, it's a lot of fun, it's fun for me, I get my feelings off through my music, but listen, you got your life wrapped up in it, and it's very difficult to come out here and lay something down when people . . ."

For a few moments, she appeared lost in her own reveries, but then found her confidence once more. "It's like last Sunday," she said. "I went to a Hopi ceremonial dance in the desert, and there were a lot of people there, and there were tourists, and there were tourists who were getting into it like Indians, and there were Indians who were getting into it like tourists, and I think that you're acting like tourists, man! Give us some respect!" She played a few more songs. The booing softened some but continued nonetheless.

It might have been the ruckus onstage, or the tantalizing messages on the fences, or the mere physics of so many bodies under pressure, but by the time Mitchell waved her curt goodbyes and trotted backstage, the fences had begun to collapse. By the midafternoon, with Miles Davis's furious blows providing the perfect sound track to anarchy, Farr had received reports that there were now nearly six hundred thousand people crammed into East Afton Farm. There was no point in ordering more toilets now, an assistant said ruefully; no number of commodes the production could reasonably procure would satisfy the demand. The same was true for trash cans, security guards, water troughs. The only thing to do now, the assistant concluded, was hope for peace.

But Farr was raging. With just over 10 percent of the audience having purchased a ticket, he had no way of paying anyone he had engaged, from artists to electricians. Even if the festival concluded without further eruptions, he would still face years of lawsuits, and, most likely, bankruptcy. He waited for Tiny Tim to conclude his strange act—it ended with a ghostly rendition of "There'll Always Be an England" belted out through a megaphone—stomped onto the stage, and made an announcement.

"There's a nonintelligent element that seems to think that

they could have a fun little game and cause trouble and make a name for themselves," he bellowed. "They will be treated with the contempt they deserve, and if they try to get in through the mud they'll go out through the mud, but on their chins." With this he introduced Kris Kristofferson.

The country singer, wearing a black turtleneck, took the microphone slowly. The festival had been a bad trip. Since his first aborted performance three days earlier, Kristofferson had spent time hanging around backstage and talking to the other artists. Increasingly they were reporting that the crowd was turning unruly. Booing was only the beginning. Objects were now being hurled at anyone who dared step onto the stage. And, with nothing to do with their waste, the audience quickly took to setting it on fire, which meant that flaming rubbish was being thrown at the musicians as well. Since they had assailed the energetic Emerson, Lake & Palmer, how would the audience receive Kristofferson's soft country songs?

He started playing. A bottle came whirring by, hitting him on the shoulder. He stopped for a moment, then started again. Some cans rained down on his band. And then there was the shouting. And the smell of burning garbage. "We're going to do two more in spite of everything except rifle fire," Kristofferson said, not trying to hide the disdain in his voice. "I think they're going to shoot us." He decided to try his most famous song, "Me and Bobby McGee." Maybe that would soothe the mob. By the time he got to the part about freedom being "just another word for nothin' left to lose," the boos were too loud to ignore. Kristofferson stopped playing, gave the crowd the finger, and stalked offstage. Farr, slouching at stage left, did nothing to stop him. He walked slowly to the microphone. Kristofferson's musicians were still playing "Bobby McGee."

"That was Kris Kristofferson," Farr said when the music finally died down. "Now I just want you to hang on one minute. I want you to hear something, and I want you to hear it fucking good! There are some good people out here, and you are insulting their intelligence! And if you come to this country at our invitation, and we have to charge you, through no choice of our own, three pounds, if you don't want to pay it, don't fucking well come!"

Nothing but boos. The Who took the stage.

Somewhere in the audience, Mick Farren, having returned to the Isle of Wight, was looking on at the spectacle of contempt, amazed. Like most of the excitable young men in his political circles, he thought a lot about revolution and very little about its aftermath. He was thrilled when hundreds of thousands stormed down Desolation Hill and crashed the festival, but shocked when he saw them attacking the artists, shouting at one another, and setting their own feces on fire. Somewhere on the grass he'd seen a young man feed his toddler a few drops of acid. He tried talking to him but was called an "oppressive fascist pig." Nobody listened. Everybody shoved.

With no one in control of the crowd, the artists themselves stepped up. Sly and the Family Stone tried to appeal to their fans and ask for quiet, but they were soon rebuked by another militant jumping onstage and speechifying and by another downpour of bottles and cans. Mungo Jerry refused to leave his trailer and canceled his set. The Doors took the stage but, fearing projectiles, instructed their roadies to turn off all the lights. They played in the dark for nearly two hours, and their sepulchral music, emanating from the black emptiness onstage, drove the mob into a frenzy. The audience wanted to see Jim Morrison, so they tried to burn down the stage.

By the time Jimi Hendrix came on, they succeeded. It was after midnight, and Hendrix was wearing tight orange pants and a pink-and-yellow tie-dye shirt, looking like a flame himself. Something, probably a makeshift Molotov cocktail, had hit the scaffolding above his head, and soon it caught on fire. This seemed to amuse Hendrix. He held his Stratocaster guitar as if it were a machine gun, pointed it at the crowd, and fretted fast. The riffs were high-pitched, difficult to take. A few security guards rushed onto the stage to try and put out the fire, and their walkie-talkies interfered with the amplifier's frequency. The howling of Hendrix's guitar flickered, sounding otherworldly. In three weeks' time, the musician—ravaged by stress and sleeping pills—would asphyxiate on his own vomit in a friend's basement flat in Notting Hill, but that night on Wight he seemed more exuberant than he'd been in months. He played faster and faster, and anyone in the audience who was in possession of a lighter flicked his thumb on the flint and went searching for something to burn.

Leaning back against a loudspeaker, Rikki Farr watched Hendrix play. He made no effort to stop the fire or calm the crowd. He was paralyzed. He had given all the speeches he could give, tried all the tricks he knew, done everything in his power to get everyone to settle down and everything under control. Earlier that evening he had taken the microphone one last time, told the audience exactly how much the festival had cost and how much money he still needed to raise, and pleaded with them to pay whatever they could to help him cover his expenses. No one did. Walking aimlessly backstage, Farr felt many things. He felt angry with the hooligans who took two days to destroy a festival he'd spent a year putting together. He was devastated to see so many of his peers swept by the deluge of violence and squalor. He was distraught because he realized that there would never again be another festival like the one on Wight. But mainly, he told a filmmaker who happened to be interviewing him at that moment, he just felt a lot older. He shuffled off to his tent and went to sleep.

But the festival wasn't over yet. There were still a few more hours, and still one more act: Leonard Cohen. One of Farr's assistants went to look for Cohen, and found him sleeping in his trailer. He woke him up and asked him to take the stage as soon as possible. As he watched Cohen get dressed, producer Bob Johnston was nervous. Having Cohen play Wight had been his idea. He'd produced for Elvis and Cash and Dylan, and he thought he knew a good opportunity when he saw one, but watching the fire and the fury unleashed on the English island made him doubt his judgment. He had hoped this would be Leonard Cohen's breakout concert, his first show in front of a truly huge audience; now Johnston just prayed that Cohen would survive it unharmed. It almost seemed unlikely: Ever since the two of them left New York for a brief European tour, backed by an eclectic band of musicians, violence struck at every turn. In Paris some fans got a bit too close. In Berlin someone pulled a gun. At some point along the rowdy tour, Cohen had dubbed his ragtag band the Army.

He, however, was not much of a warrior. A decade older than most of the other musicians at the festival, he shared none of their affectations or appetites. Some in his entourage wondered why he bothered at all with the whole rock-and-roll lifestyle. Judy Collins, who came backstage to say hello, told a few embarrassing stories about him, like a mother showing nude baby photos of her now-grown child. A few years back, she said, she had invited Cohen up onstage to sing "Suzanne," the hit song he'd written for her. He made it halfway through before turning his back to the audience and sprinting offstage. He had to be cajoled back and begged to finish his song. Johnston told a similar story. Recording his first album three years earlier, Cohen engaged the producer John Simon, impressed with the work Simon had done with the Band. The two, Johnston recalled, soon fought bitterly—Simon was so frustrated with Cohen's refusal to use a rhythm section that he abandoned the production and allowed Cohen to finish it as he saw fit. Which wasn't much solace to Cohen: Well aware that most of the musicians engaged to accompany him mocked his lack of experience and felt no love for his gloomy melodies, he preferred to record his own tracks alone in the studio, singing and playing guitar by himself and allowing the sound engineers to retroactively wed his work to that of the other musicians. The members of the Army had no trouble believing the stories: Cohen was polite but aloof, professional but inscrutable. He almost never hung out, and when he did there was little in common to talk about. While most of his musicians had spent the decade searching for the next gig, the next fix, the next fuck, Cohen had been in self-imposed exile in a two-story beachfront cottage on the Greek island of Hydra, writing poetry. When the stage at Wight was set ablaze, members of the Army joined the other artists backstage in feverish discussions of the potential threat to their well-being. Cohen just turned to Bob Johnston, and—with what the producer thought was the beginning of a smile—said, "Wake me up when it's time, Bob. I'm going to take a nap over there, by the fire."

Now, watching Cohen get dressed, Johnston felt a pulsating fear thudding inside him. He peeked out of the trailer and saw Kris Kristofferson, Joan Baez, and Judy Collins lounging backstage, waiting for their friend to play his show. Cohen, Johnston thought, was nowhere near as tough as Kristofferson, not as determined as Baez, not as well respected as Collins, and if the three of them were pelted with bottles and booed offstage, what chance did Cohen have? But Cohen himself showed no sign of concern. He put on a black T-shirt and a safari jacket, and—unshaved, hair unkempt—walked up onto the stage. He said nothing to the members of the Army. His face, some of them thought, was blank.

"Greetings," Cohen said into the microphone, "greetings." His tone was casual, his voice soft. He continued, "When I was seven years old," he said in that same mellow way, "my father used to take me to the circus. He had a black mustache, and a great vest, and a pansy in his lapel, and he liked the circus better than I did."

Sitting a few feet behind Cohen, Charlie Daniels, a young fiddler Bob Johnston had brought along from Nashville, was amused. Years later, recalling how he felt at that moment, he said he just couldn't believe Cohen was trying to tell six hundred thousand people a goddamn bedtime story. But, in a near-monotone, Cohen continued.

"There was one thing at the circus that happened that I always used to wait for," he said. "I don't want to impose on you, this isn't like a sing-along, but there was one moment when a man would stand up and say, would everybody light a match so we could locate one another? And could I ask you, each person, to light a match, so that I could see where you all are? Could each of you light a match, so that you'll sparkle like fireflies, each at your different heights? I would love to see those matches flare."

The audience obeyed. For five days the men and women onstage—organizers, artists, or anarchists—had been talking at them. Cohen was talking *to* them. He seemed like one of them. He seemed to care. Slowly they took out matches and lighters, and instead of setting things on fire they waved their arms in the air, emitting light and heat. Cohen smiled. "Oh, yeah!" he said softly. "Oh, yeah. Now I know that you know why you're lighting them." He strummed a few chords on the guitar, and continued his speech, half singing: "It's good to be here alone in front of six hundred thousand people. It's a large nation but it's still weak. Still very weak. It needs to get a lot stronger before it can claim a right to land."

These were heavy words for two in the morning, but they seemed to permeate. Cohen wasn't just telling the audience to stop rioting; he was about to give them an alternative. Playing as slowly as he could, Cohen began with one of his most famous songs: "Like . . . a . . . bird . . . on . . . the . . . wire. . . ." Whoever was still standing now sat down on the grass and listened.

When the song ended the audience clapped. Not thunderously, but still. A handful, still hopped up on the adrenaline of the afternoon, booed, but they were soon subdued. The six hundred thousand wanted to hear what Cohen had to say.

What he had to say was poetry. He had started out as a

poet, and his first public performances consisted of reciting verse in small, smoky Montreal coffeehouses. He might as well have been in one when he stared into the distance (in the way that poets sometimes do when they're reading out loud) and began his soliloquy.

"I wrote this in a peeling room in the Chelsea Hotel, before I was rich and famous and they gave me well-painted rooms," he said. "I was coming off of amphetamines, and I was pursuing a blond lady whom I met in a Nazi poster. And I was doing many things to attract her attention. I was lighting wax candles in the form of men and women. I was marrying the smoke of two cones of sandalwood." Then he started playing another of his songs, "One of Us Cannot Be Wrong."

To Murray Lerner, a middle-aged filmmaker from New York whose camera crews had documented every moment of the festival, the effect was hypnotic. Throughout five days of performances, he'd been too busy shouting out orders to stop and listen to the music. But Cohen's words made him put down his camera and look up at the man onstage. Cohen, Lerner thought, looked like someone who might do your taxes, not like someone who could stir your soul. Two hours earlier Lerner had been packing up his equipment, certain that the fires and the violence would lead to a massive stampede. He had been ready to run for shelter. But now everything was still, and Lerner had no idea how Leonard Cohen had pulled it off. Standing beside Lerner, Joan Baez was equally baffled. "People say that a song needs to make sense," she told the filmmaker. "Leonard proves otherwise. It doesn't necessarily make sense at all, it just comes from so deep inside of him, it somehow touches deep down inside other people. I'm not sure how it works, but I know that it works." Lerner nodded in agreement as he listened. It reminded him of something he'd once read T. S. Eliot say of Dante—that the genius of poetry was that it communicated before it was understood.

Onstage, Cohen was done with the ephemera. He was smiling. He turned to his bandmates frequently now, nodding his head encouragingly or saying a kind word or two. In his confidence, he decided it was time to speak honestly. He played a few basic chords and delivered a short speech-song.

"They gave me some money," he sang, "for my sad and famous song. They said the crowd is waiting, hurry up or they'll be gone. But I could not change my style, and I guess I never will. So I sing this for the poison snakes on Devastation Hill." And then came a noisy, joyous rendition of "Diamonds in the Mine," with Charlie Daniels singeing the strings and Bob Johnston, playing piano, pounding happily on the keys.

"He's taking them on," said Kris Kristofferson, standing a few feet away with Lerner and Baez. "He's taking the fuckers right on."

Cohen was. He had renamed Desolation Hill "Devastation Hill," and called its occupants poison snakes. As he did, however, the poison snakes—the ones who crawled in through the mud or slung themselves at the fences, the ones who slithered onto the stage to spit out venomous messages, the ones who set the evil fires—they just huddled together and listened. Kristofferson felt something like elation. He clapped along madly.

It was nearly four in the morning by the time Cohen was ready to end his set. He had played all of his hits, and launched into a few more bits of poetry. Someone in the crowd screamed a request, asking Cohen to sing "Seems So Long Ago, Nancy."

Cohen signaled to his band that he'd like to play that one by himself. "It was in 1961," he said, and then spoke of the woman in the song. "She went into the bathroom and blew her head [off] with her brother's shotgun." He pointed at the audience, now lying down, cuddled on top of one another on the grass. "In those days," he continued, "there wasn't that kind of horizontal support. She was right where you are now but there was no one else around to light their matches." He played the song, and when he was finished he put down his guitar.

The introductory chapters of rock biographies all end this way, with a crystalline moment of transformation in which an artist finally finds his voice and becomes who he'd been meant to be his entire life. That wasn't the case with Cohen. He'd found some self-confidence, maybe, and some calm, but, taking the stage, Cohen was the same person he'd been all along. The six hundred thousand who heard him that night—they were the ones transformed.

"I know it's been cold and I know it's been damp," he said. "I know you've been sick all night long. But let's renew ourselves now. Let's renew ourselves now. Let's renew ourselves now. Good night." And off the stage he went.

CHAPTER ONE

"Looking for the Note"

L ife as Leonard Norman Cohen knew it ended on January 14, 1944, the day his father died. That morning, he and his sister Esther, five years his senior, walked past the dead man's coffin, taking one last look at his round, alabaster face. It was Esther's birthday, and when they returned home, Leonard, now the man of the house, told his sister that a celebration was in order. A birthday was a birthday, and there was protocol to be followed. For a moment, they tried to be happy, acting as if nothing else had happened. But every thought led them back to the funeral home, to the high, cold forehead and the lifeless lips. They started sobbing. Esther was fourteen; Leonard was nine.

For a few days he did his best to carry on. The rules of the house, crafted with care by Nathan Cohen when he was alive, were still rigidly observed—the shoes lined up neatly in front of the beds each night, pressed jackets or ironed dresses worn to the dinner table every evening—carrying on the affectations of a lieutenant in the Fourth Field Company of Canadian Engineers who dreamed of one day seeing his son in uniform. But the inertia of discipline wasn't enough to keep emotions at bay. Everything about the mourning rites of adults seemed designed to help the bereaved ease into the future, but Leonard wanted a few more moments with the past. One night he sneaked into Nathan's room and selected his father's favorite bow tie. With a pair of scissors he cut a slit in the fabric, then scribbled a few words on a slip of paper and inserted it into the tie. Quietly he walked down the great staircase and opened the front door of the house. He tiptoed his way to the backyard, which abutted King George Park. With the tall locust trees as his dark and silent witnesses, Leonard dug into the frozen earth, tossed the tie into the hole, and covered it with dirt. "It was the first thing I wrote," he told *People* magazine many years later. "I've been digging in the garden for years, looking for it. Maybe that's all I'm doing, looking for the note."[1]

He wasn't speaking allegorically, or at least not entirely. That night in the garden Cohen became not just a writer, but a particular kind of writer—the kind who wrote and then destroyed his work. At nine he understood instinctively what Kafka, who ordered his manuscripts burned, or the great Jewish mystic and storyteller, Rabbi Nachman of Breslov, who did the same, had labored a lifetime to learn: that sometimes, if you're sincere about what you have to say, if you want to communicate the full force of human emotions like grief and longing and gratitude, you try writing and then realize that your words are just as transient as you are, that they always fail you when you need them most, and that if they can't serve their purpose and convey meaning perfectly—if they can't reach the unborn and the dead—then they're better off buried or burned.[2] It would take Cohen decades to learn what to do with this early, piercing insight. All he could do that night in

1944 was head back to his room and try to make sense of his world as it now stood.

It was, almost entirely, a Jewish world, its inhabitants leading the kind of life—free, ripe with rights, removed from tradition—that millennia's worth of their ancestors could have never imagined. Like all other wealthy Jewish families in Montreal, the Cohens lived on top of the hill, in Westmount, having climbed their way up from humble beginnings in the foundries and factories and sweatshops downtown. They helped build a three-thousand-seat leviathan of a synagogue where men wore top hats to services and paid small fortunes for a premium spot in the pews. By the time Nathan Cohen and his siblings— the first generation born and raised in North America—joined the family business, wealth no longer surprised or delighted the Cohens. They lived according to the dictates of their class, with drivers and cooks and Catholic nannies for their children. And they displayed that easygoing affability that history's winners have always affected in an effort to convince themselves and others that their good fortune wasn't just a stroke of luck but the inevitable and natural order of things.

Except for Nathan Cohen. His body had been shattered in the First World War, and his afflictions leisurely killed him, over the course of years. In the meantime he grudgingly took his spot in the family's back row. While his brothers lived their lives in public, in the front office of the factory and in the front seats of the synagogue, he wheezed on the production floor, overseeing machines. Remembering his father decades after his passing, Leonard recalled "the persecuted brother, the near-poet, the innocent of machine toys, the sighing judge who listens but does not sentence," a broken man who died "spitting blood, wondering why he wasn't president of the synagogue."[3]

It was from his father's position on the totem pole, then, that teenage Leonard was invited to join the family enterprise. A summer spent hanging coats in the factory confirmed that while there was a place for him in the Cohens' constellation of privilege, it was far from the center and exuded a self-congratulatory sense of charity, of concerned uncles rescuing their hapless brother's helpless son. Besides, life in the textile business offered earthly rewards, but little that appealed to a young man who was growing up and discovering Byron and Blake.

And the prophets: Several years after his father's death Leonard's maternal grandfather moved into the spacious home on Belmont Avenue, staying for a spell and occupying the room down the hall from Leonard. Rabbi Solomon Klinitsky-Klein was a celebrated scholar who was known as Sar haDikdook, or the Prince of Grammarians. He was the author of fastidious works like *A Treasury of Rabbinic Interpretations* and *Lexicon of Hebrew Homonyms*, which he was rumored to have written without once consulting reference books. To his young grandson, however, he offered more fiery stuff—with intense concentration, he would read out loud lines like the one from Isaiah about how the Lord "shall smite the earth: with the rod of his mouth, and with the breath of his lips shall he slay the wicked."[4] This was a vision of Judaism radically different from the polite theology on offer at the Cohens' Conservative synagogue; its language of punishment and justice, of damnation and salvation, was not the sort that the gentlemen in the top hats spoke fluently.

The divide between the Cohens and Klinistsky-Klein had not always been so stark. The renowned rabbi and Lazarus Cohen, Leonard's great-grandfather, were both born in Lithuania, both considered promising Talmudic scholars, and both selected to teach at the finest Hebrew schools. Poverty and the pogroms propelled both men to emigrate, first to England and then to Canada. Klinitsky-Klein kept up with his spiritual pursuits, establishing himself as a rabbi. Lazarus Cohen had earthlier aspirations, starting off as a clerk at a lumberyard and struggling through a succession of businesses built on brawn, from a foundry to a dredging company, until he'd amassed enough wealth to take his place among Montreal's mightiest.

With his long white beard and stricken look, Lazarus bore an uncanny resemblance to El Greco's portrait of Saint Jerome—both come off as men who reserve their best conversations for the angels. The synagogue he helped build quickly became Montreal's most vaunted. The name Cohen and his cofounders chose for their congregation said everything about their aspirations: Shaar Hashomayim, the Gate of Heaven. Its founders, strongly affiliated with their city's well-off English-speaking Episcopalians, gleefully embraced the British mannerisms of their neighbors and designed a crest for their shul, a blue-and-gold ornament topped by a winged Torah scroll and emblazoned with the synagogue's motto—"This is none other than the house of God, and this is the gate of heaven."

Such grandeur placed a significant burden on the next generation of Cohens, and Lazarus's son, Lyon, did not disappoint. He had his father's gift for commerce, and started the clothing business that would soon make the Cohen clan an even greater fortune. A friend of Klinitsky-Klein's from back in Lithuania, Lyon was happy to see the rabbi's daughter, Masha, marry his son Nathan. It was not uncommon for Jewish families thriving in the new world to think sentimentally about the old one they had left behind, and welcoming the renowned rabbi into their extended family must have pleased the Cohens, injecting their increasingly assimilated lives with a core of traditional values and beliefs.

And so it was on the cusp of old and new, between ancient texts and modern buildings, with one grandfather looking heavenward and the other toiling here on earth, that Leonard Cohen grew up. But without a strong parental figure to guide him firmly in either direction, the young boy was left to seek answers on his own. And the question that consumed him—the one he could not, as a boy, eloquently express but that went on to guide his career and inform his art and forge his world-view—was the same one that shaped the course of Judaism in the twentieth century, namely how, with the old religious ties loosened and the ancient communal bonds unmade, one was to find any meaning in life.

To the extent that this question has distinct origins, they belong not in the dense and scholarly pages of history but on the hazier horizon of biblical accounts, at the moment when the Israelites, freshly out of Egypt, gather at the foot-hills of Mount Sinai to await word from Moses, their leader, who has traveled up the mountain to meet his God. But God is gnomic. "And ye shall be unto me a kingdom of priests," he says, "and an holy nation."[5] And with that, he sends the newly chosen people on their way. Queries, of course, abound: Why, the dust-covered nomads, huddled in anticipation, might be forgiven for asking, were we the ones chosen, and not, say, a mighty empire like Egypt? Might we one day become unchosen, and, if so, for which transgressions? Does the compact hold with our children after us? Does it hold in perpetuity? And, most important, having been chosen, what is it that we were chosen to do? God never says. To have been chosen means having to spend eternity wondering what it means to have been chosen.

It's a terrific cosmic joke, but it makes for great theology, too. Exiled for millennia, scattered across all corners of the world, the Jews have survived as a nation, outliving so many of antiquity's proudest peoples, because they had these strange questions to ponder: Why us? And what now? These questions fashioned a religion that gave them the license to mix with their neighbors—after all, whatever the chosen ones' mission may be, it probably had to do with humanity at large—but also compelled them to remain somewhat exclusively ingathered, as the chosen people would not remain a distinct people for long if they wholeheartedly adopted the customs of the gentiles, ate their dishes, and married their daughters and sons. One day, the rabbis promised, it would all become clear: One day the messiah will come, and the Jews will return to the Promised Land. One day, but not yet. In the meantime, they warned their flock against taking matters into their own hands and trying to pave their own path to redemption. There was nothing the Jews could do but wait, the rabbis advised, but while they waited, there were plenty of things they could do, from the ethical treatment of animals to the establishment of just courts, all detailed in the Torah and all designed to make life on earth a bit more heavenly. With time, the Jewish messiah, too, emerged as another cosmic joke: He will only arrive, Jewish theology insists, when all Jews are pious and compassionate and ready to receive him, but when all Jews are pious and compassionate and kind to one another, there will be no need for a messiah.[6]

With few exceptions, this holding pattern worked well for the Jews. At points some turned to self-proclaimed prophets, and others abandoned the faith altogether. When things got very tough—as they did in the eighteenth and nineteenth centuries, with one pogrom after another claiming lives and shaking communities—Hasidism arose and offered its adherents a direct and ecstatic channel to God through prayer and meditation, as well as the benefits of powerful rabbis to follow and consult. But the principles of the religion remained more or less unchanged. And then came the Emancipation.

Beginning in 1791 in France and quickly spreading across Europe, Jews were relieved of the old edicts that kept them from being recognized as equal citizens in their countries of residence. In rapid succession, nation after nation afforded its Jews the right to vote and run for office, allowed them new freedoms of occupation, and welcomed them into new and previously inaccessible circles. In return the Jews were expected to assimilate, to shed their old-world religion and become modern. As the princess Halm-Eberstein observed of the young and ambitious Jews coming out from under tradition's yoke in George Eliot's *Daniel Deronda*, the newly emancipated "wanted to live a large life, with freedom to do what every one else did."[7]

But the old spiritual skin was impossible to shed. Millennia's worth of convictions and rituals don't just disappear. They linger and lurk, seeking a crack through which they can once again slip into consciousness. Freud, a second-generation emancipated Jew, had something similar in mind when he spoke of the return of the repressed. Many of the newly emancipated found refuge in Zionism, a movement that wrapped the luminous and ancient messianic expectations in the plain brown paper of nationalism. Marxists and militarists, rabbis and fierce secularists, men who defined Judaism as a culture and men who were convinced it was an ethnicity—all gathered under Zionism's banner. They yearned to fulfill the prophecy of resettling the Promised Land, even if they couldn't agree on what kind of polity might emerge once the Jews returned and established a modern nation-state of their own. In their zeal they cast aside the old rabbinical exhortations to do nothing but wait. The messiah, they scoffed, could come whenever he so wished, but in the meantime there was no reason not to act, to work the land, to revive the ancient language heretofore used only in prayer. All of Zionism's internal contradictions, all the divisions that set one faction apart from another, were erased by the enthusiasm generated by the faint promise that the Jews could finally come back home.

That enthusiasm moved the Cohens: Four years before the First Zionist Congress convened in Basel in 1897 and declared as its aim "establishing for the Jewish people a publicly and legally assured home in Palestine," Lazarus Cohen had already visited the land and purchased parts of it in the hope of future settlement. His son, Lyon, inherited his father's passions; the door of his mansion in Westmount—where interior lives were kept hidden by stone walls and muted sensibilities—was carved with a large Star of David. In 1919, Lyon became a founding member and the first president of the Canadian Jewish Congress, uniting Canada's disparate Jewish organizations.

The inaugural conference, held at Montreal's City Hall, was addressed by the nation's solicitor general. In a bit of ceremony, Cohen produced a large flag with the Star of David emblazoned on it, and used it to cover the mayor's chair. It was a perfect metaphor for the new organization's dual intentions—the conference's two major decisions addressed the need to settle newly arrived Jewish immigrants to Canada, mainly by setting up communities in the western parts of the country, as well as the importance of following up on the Balfour Declaration and pursuing a Jewish homeland in Palestine. With one eye trained on affairs at home and another looking east, to Zion, the Cohens thrived.

Zionism, however, was not the only contender for the passions of Jews unmoored by the Emancipation. Jewish mysticism beckoned, too: As Gershom Scholem, probably its greatest scholar, argued, mysticism has always fought an uphill battle against the steely rationality of the halacha, or Jewish law. Scholem traced the origins of the kabbalah, the Jewish mystical school of thought, to the same medieval period that also witnessed the rise of great and astute scholars who spent lifetimes parsing the letter of the law, like Moses Maimonides. The twelfth-century rabbi's best-known work, *The Guide for the Perplexed*, is meticulous, combining textual analysis, Aristotelian cosmology, and rational philosophy. At its core is staunch adherence to negative theology, or the idea that there are no positive and definitive statements we can make about God. Can we say God exists? Maimonides argues that the best we can do is say that he doesn't *not* exist. Can we say that he is omniscient? No, but we can argue that he's not ignorant. He's not ours to know, and certainly not for us to see: He's an abstraction. Which, of course, makes for tremendous intellectual fun—Maimonides greatly influenced Thomas Aquinas—but is not a great way to move the spirit. Human beings, the earliest mystics understood, worship with their hearts just as much as with their minds. They frequently feel the need to abandon reason and revel in the mysterious and the ecstatic and the obscure. That, in part, was the appeal of the Hebrew prophets: More than just advocating for social justice, they offered a stark alternative to the cool and critical strand of scholarship Judaism has always championed. They were poets, and none more than Isaiah, with his vision of swords turning into plowshares. The prophets shouted. They trembled. They felt with all their hearts.

Maimonides found such intensity detrimental. He could not ignore the role prophecy had played in the Jewish tradition, but he did attempt to radically redefine it. "It is one of the basic principles of religion that God inspires men with the prophetic gift," he wrote. "But the spirit of prophecy only rests upon the wise man who is distinguished by great wisdom and strong moral character, whose passions never overcome him in anything whatsoever, but who by his rational faculty always has his passions under control, and possesses a broad and sedate mind." The prophet, the great scholar added, must also be "physically sound."[8]

Strength, discipline, industriousness—these were the virtues the Cohens had always promoted, the character traits that had made them great merchants and good soldiers. Young Leonard was expected to follow suit, expected not only to join the family business but also to adopt the kind of dispassionate Maimonidean approach that was all the rage at Shaar

Hashomayim, an approach that believed a man was measured by his deeds alone, not by his thoughts. But there was something about Klinitsky-Klein's readings of Isaiah that Leonard couldn't shake off. He understood them, he told a biographer decades later, to be a manifestation of his grandfather's "confrontational, belligerent stance"[9] against Judaism's polite rationality. The old man read and reread the prophet's stirring passages rather than worship with the dull and the flightless who made up so much of the Jewish community around him.

Even though he lived with his daughter and her children for less than a year, Klinitsky-Klein gave his grandson the gift of an alternative, and far more stirring, vision of Jewish life. It was spiritual but also deeply erotic: Isaiah's soul may have pointed heavenward, but his tongue was earthy, speaking of sinners as "the seed of the adulterer and the whore" and equating those who had strayed off the righteous path with a woman who has "uncovered" herself "to another than me."[10] The prophet understood that humankind's spiritual and sexual yearnings were intertwined. It was an insight that found a ready listener in the adolescent Cohen, himself discovering both yearnings at the same time.

But what was an adolescent—his father dead, his mother gnawed by grief and anxiety, his own future unclear—to do with such an insight? The only way to quiet the chorus of demons that rattled Cohen with emotions too great for him to handle was to engage in the teenage tradition of excessive distraction: He ran for student government, mastered public speaking, learned to play a host of instruments passably, rode his bicycle, played sports, toyed with hypnosis, pursued women, served as a summer camp counselor, and organized events and activities wherever he went. Observed from afar, Cohen gave off such an affable and adroit air that some of those who knew him during this period could be forgiven for thinking, as they did, that he had willed himself into erasing whatever traumatic marks his father's passing might have left on his psyche and emerged a new and whole man. He did no such thing. At home he would spend most of his time locked in his room, hiding, reading. And he developed a lifelong habit of wandering, setting out on hours-long excursions that led him to the gritty parts of town that most of his fellow young Westmount Jews had no idea existed. It was freedom, but it came at a cost. While his friends took hesitant steps into maturity, buttressed by families and a sense of security, Cohen had few boundaries to impede or shape his explorations. He could walk downtown. He could hypnotize the young housekeeper into removing her underwear. He could stay up past dawn. As long as his grades were good, as long as he kept up appearances, he could run wild. He wasn't particularly close to his sister, and his mother had remarried and then divorced; she comes off in her son's recollections as doting and emotional, caring but quick to lay on the guilt. Often she would stay up all night worrying about Leonard, and then, when he came back from his strolls, yell at him, hug him, and offer to cook him some eggs. She didn't know how to guide him to comfort. He had to find his own way.

CHAPTER TWO

The Soul of Canada

He found poetry. How he did isn't important. In later years he was repeatedly asked for an origin story, and repeatedly gave contradictory, often playful answers. Sometimes he would claim to have been sitting on a deck and basking in the sun when, out of nowhere, a poem struck him like a ray and announced to him his destiny as a conduit for divine inspiration. Other times he would take a more earthly—and earthy—tone and say he only started writing to get girls. "I wanted them and I couldn't have them," he told an interviewer in 1970. "That's really how I started writing poetry. I wrote notes to women so as to have them. They began to show them around and soon people started calling it poetry. When it didn't work with women, I appealed to God."[1]

While he remained coy about the poetry he wrote, Cohen was much more forthcoming about the poetry he read. Here an origin story does exist, singular and undisputed, confirmed in interviews and public appearances: When Cohen was fifteen, he took one of his ambles and ended up in a used-book shop, where he stumbled upon a copy of a book of poetry by

Federico García Lorca. The Spaniard couldn't have asked for a better reader than Cohen: Astutely, Cohen realized right away that Lorca's central artistic engine was also his own. It was the *duende*.

The term is hard to translate. It is frequently referred to as "deep song," and often just as "soul." In a lecture he gave in 1922, Lorca defined it as "a stammer, a wavering emission of the voice, a marvelous buccal undulation that smashes the resonant cells of our tempered scale, eludes the cold, rigid staves of modern music, and makes the tightly closed flowers of the semi-tones blossom into a thousand petals."[2] But *duende* wasn't just for musicians; it was also the dowry of poets who cared to apply "the finest degrees of Sorrow and Pain, in the service of the purest, most exact expression."[3] *Duende*—to paraphrase another of its famous celebrants, Goethe—is that profound and nebulous sadness we all feel but can't easily articulate. In Lorca, Cohen glimpsed his own state of mind, reflected back at him in beautiful verse, rich with intricate imagery, elegant and gloomy. Often—another attraction for the rabbi's dutiful grandson—Lorca looked heavenward in his attempt, in a sort of emotional alchemy, to turn misery into joy. He wrote of figures like the "brown Christ" who passes "from the lily of Judea / to the carnation of Spain,"[4] a universal redeemer who pays little attention to cultural, historical, or religious distinctions.

With Lorca by his side, Cohen was ready to try his own hand at writing poetry. On the cover of one early notebook, he scribbled "poems written while dying of love." He was out looking for *duende*, but soon realized that a gargantuan hurdle separated him from everything he deemed poetic: Unlike

Lorca, a gay artist who claimed to have Gypsy blood, collaborated with Luis Buñuel and Salvador Dalí, and was murdered by the fascists while fighting in Spain's civil war, Cohen lived in a tony neighborhood in a cold country where people were primarily interested in their work and passed the time going to the movies or listening to Patti Page on the radio. It was hardly an environment conducive to romantic life. Spain quivered with flamenco; where was the soul of Canada?

It wasn't a theoretical question. By the time Cohen graduated from high school and entered Montreal's McGill University, in 1951, the English Department, in whose halls he took a great number of his classes, was teeming with students struggling to reinvent Canadian literature.

Or, rather, invent it. In *Survival*, her seminal history of the subject, Margaret Atwood noted with bemused horror that when she traveled across Canada and told people that she was writing a book on Canadian literature, "the two questions I was asked most frequently by audience members were, 'Is there any Canadian literature?' and 'Supposing there is, isn't it just a second-rate copy of *real* literature, which comes from England and the United States?'"[5]

Of course there were novels and poems published in Canada long before Leonard Cohen first wrote a word, many of them outstanding. But as Canada itself was little more than a handful of provinces and religions and languages and traditions struggling to congeal into a unified nation, whatever literary works were produced in Canada failed to fall into a common mosaic that, seen from above, might resemble a national literature. Until the middle of the twentieth century,

Canada's literary output consisted mainly of long disquisitions on nature and humankind's slim odds of surviving it, as well as subtle but consistent expressions of the idea, common to all budding colonial literatures, that, as Atwood put it, "the Great Good Place was, culturally speaking, elsewhere."[6]

Elsewhere was down south, and down south the poets and the thinkers—many of them born into pious households and stirred by intimations of the divine—saw the savage beauty of their land as a source of infinite bounty. This was a major theme with Emerson and the Transcendentalists; Canadians, however, were more skeptical. To them nature was a mindless, hungry beast. "I have long been impressed in Canadian poetry by a tone of deep terror in regard to nature," wrote Northrop Frye, the renowned Canadian critic. "It is not a terror of the dangers or discomforts or even the mysteries of nature, but a terror of soul at something that these things manifest. The human mind has nothing but human and moral values to cling to if it is to preserve its integrity or even its sanity, yet the vast unconsciousness of nature in front of it seems an unanswerable denial of those values."[7]

Whatever the reasons for these diverging worldviews, while American literature thrived, Canada waited for its Emersons and Thoreaus. As late as the 1920s and 1930s, as American poets like T. S. Eliot and Ezra Pound forged the modernist moment by testing the elasticity of language and form, their Canadian counterparts took much more hesitant steps out of their Victorian sensibilities. Even E. J. Pratt, the nation's greatest poet, is best known for two epic poems—1940's *Brébeuf and His Brethren*, about a Jesuit martyr, and 1952's *Towards the Last Spike*, about the building of Canada's transcontinental railroad—that are more celebrated for their adherence to historical records than they are for challenging the conventions of poetry.

And then came the Jews.

Two of them in particular: Irving Layton and A. M. Klein. They wrote very different poetry, Layton's exuberant and Klein's studious and pondering. But, like Emerson, they believed that "within man is the soul of the whole; the wise silence; the universal beauty, to which every part and particle is equally related, the eternal ONE."[8] When they started out, this idea was much too radical for the local, cerebral, timid sensibility: One of Klein's first poems was rejected for publication in a prestigious literary magazine because it contained the word "soul."

Klein had met Layton in 1930, when the latter was still in high school and needed tutoring in Latin. Three years Layton's senior, Klein had much in common with his rowdy student. They had both escaped the pogroms of Europe as infants and taken shelter in the Jewish ghetto of St. Urbain Street in downtown Montreal. They both found a calling early on in literature. But whereas Layton displayed the sort of fleshy rambunctiousness that came easily to a kid who grew up in an apartment beneath a brothel, Klein was raised by a devout father, considered joining the clergy, and was never too far, in his speech and thought, from the rabbinical. When he agreed to educate Layton, however, Klein taught him not the Talmud but Virgil. The two met at a soccer field not far from their old school, and Layton sat entranced as Klein's deep voice plumbed the depths of the *Aeneid*. They were both transfixed by the language and its meter, but even more with the grand narrative and its stately structure. Themselves raised on the fables of an ancient faith that saw itself as the progenitor of Western civilization, the two young Jews easily fell in love with the ancient Romans and, later, the Greeks. When Klein started a literary magazine at his university, he called it the *McGilliad*; it published Irving Layton's first poem. A decade later, when he wanted to express his disgust over the unchecked rise of Nazi Germany, Klein did so in a humorous, book-length epic poem, *The Hitleriad*.

This infusion of mythical thinking and imagery into the staid core of Canadian poetry greatly appealed to other young poets, like Louis Dudek and F. R. Scott, and for the first time produced not a loose coalition of poets but an actual literary school bound by friendship and shared sensibilities. But Layton was never really one for schools, and while Klein continued to explore Jewish tradition and history, he trained his mind on more common matters. A poem from his second collection, published in 1948, is titled "To the Lawyer Handling My Divorce Case," in which the poet—then moving from wife number one to wife number two in what would ultimately be a series of five—imagines his attorney referring to him as a bit of bodily waste. "If at all," the poem begins, "he thinks of me as a soiled fingernail."[9] Other poems were equally as curious about the body and its dictates. Layton's world was still an epic place governed by spirits and demons, but it was also occupied by women who had to be courted and seduced. He was, in that respect, a student of the Hebrew prophets. Finally the frozen kingdom had a poet who wrote about fucking, and the fact that he acted out on these carnal scenarios in life as well as in verse, and the fact that he let his hair grow long and shaggy and always spoke as if he was reading poetry, soon made Layton the nation's most fascinating poet.

It also made him a professor at McGill, where in 1954 he met a promising junior, the young poet Leonard Cohen. As a thinker Cohen probably learned more from Klein, whose best works are dense with ideas and allusions to rituals, and as a teacher of craft, Cohen had Dudek, who introduced him not only to the history of verse but also to its rules. These are necessary skills for anyone interested in writing poetry. But how is a twenty-year-old to learn how to be a poet? There was more to the calling than the scrubbing of lines. There was the *duende*, and it hardly lived in Westmount. Cohen wrote poetry, but he wasn't ready to appoint himself a member of the same club as Lorca and the others he admired. In his junior year at McGill, as the newly elected president of the debate club, he traveled with his friends to the Norfolk Penitentiary outside Boston to debate the inmates about the moral implications of television on society. He had already published some of his writing in school publications, and someone introduced him as a poet. When he took the podium, he denied the allegation. "My colleague has promised you a poet," he said, "but I am afraid that you will be disappointed. I do not converse in rhyming couplets, nor do I wear a cape or walk brooding over the moor or drink wine from a polished human skull or stride frequently into the cosmic night. I am never discovered sitting amid Gothic ruins in moonlight clutching in my pale hand a dying medieval lily and sighing over virgins with bosoms heaving like the sea. In fact I wouldn't recognize a dying medieval lily if I fell over one, and hardly think I could do better with a virgin, and I'll drink out of anything that has a bottom to it."[10]

Still, he wrote poetry. From his maternal grandfather he inherited the sense that the highest form of literature speaks of justice and aims at transcendence. From Layton he got a license to lust for thighs and breasts. Klein infused him with a love of the epic, and Lorca with a passion for universal truth. These gifts were all seminal, but they alone don't account for the collection of poems Cohen eventually produced, published in 1956 and aptly called *Let Us Compare Mythologies*. Like his elders, Cohen conjured otherworldly images, biblical references, spiritual currents. But these all came crashing down onto the streets of 1950s Montreal, and the sacred became all the more startling when viewed against the backdrop of the profane.

Writing about Cohen's technique years later, the novelist Michael Ondaatje called it "a gothic use of juxtaposition."[11] When Cohen, for example, described Christ as pinned "like a lovely butterfly against the wood,"[12] he recalled not the living savior but an image in a cheap painting, with "velvet wounds / and delicate twisted feet."[13] Another poem delivered another slain saint, a lady, a star of the screen, "found mutilated in a Mountain Street boarding house."[14] Her stigmata were the stab wounds streaking her chest. Yet the poem wasn't gory. It ended with young people dancing atop her grave, and with the earth blooming with fragrant roses. The martyr's death, like Christ's, was the vehicle of redemption, her mutilation a moment of beauty. Rather than lament—as is the perennial disposition of the young—the gone glories of an earlier age, and rather than compare—as was the habit of so many Canadian writers before him—his own landscape unfavorably with some other, foreign, and more luminescent one, Cohen wrote poems that argued that his own place and time were brimming with detritus but also with holiness. He realized that a simple encounter between a man and a woman was worthy of the language and the passion of the biblical prophets. Rather than try to inflate the world to epic proportions, as Layton did, Cohen made his universe seem ever grander by admitting just how awash it was with bigotry and violence and dumb lust.

It was a radical move, and not just in Canada: As he was writing his early poems, men a decade or so his elders were congregating in New York and San Francisco and forming a movement that would soon be known as the Beats. Cohen was too young to join their party, and it's just as well—they had little in common. The Beats' brightest poet, Allen Ginsberg, howled against the ravages of capitalism and offered instead a gallery of new saints—Tuli Kupferberg, Jean Genet, Blake, Rimbaud—for the hip and the young to worship. If the old religion was withering, he argued, let us sanctify a new one. It was this kind of thinking that eventually led him to found a school in Colorado for "Disembodied Poetics." But Cohen's poetics were never disembodied. He never wanted new heroes or a new faith. In his poems—and later in his song lyrics—Christ is not so much the Christian savior as he is a thin and mindful rabbi. Cohen realized that every conscientious young man from Isaiah onward looked around him and saw "the best minds" of his generation "destroyed by madness," and that the only path to real and sustainable salvation involved learning how to look at stab wounds and imagine that they just might be stigmata, to look at the ancient traditions and imagine that they were still as meaningful as ever.

"Now the hollow nests," he wrote in "The Sparrows," one of the collection's strongest poems, "sit like tumours or petrified blossoms / between the wire branches / and you, an innocent scientist / question me on these brown sparrows: / whether we should plant our yards with breadcrumbs / or mark them with the black, persistent crows / whom we hate and stone."[15]

In 1954, still a junior, Cohen handed his first draft of "The Sparrows" to his teacher Louis Dudek. The two were walking down the corridor of the English Department, and the professor stopped to read. When he was done, he asked Cohen to kneel. Using the rolled-up sheet of paper on which the poem was typed as his sword, he tapped the young man's shoulders and knighted him a poet. The poem went on to win a literary contest sponsored by the university's student newspaper, and Cohen went on to become the campus's reigning literary talent. *Let Us Compare Mythologies* was published in 1956, a few months after Cohen's graduation, the inaugural volume in a university-sponsored series of poetry books, edited by Dudek. Approximately five hundred copies were printed, all of which sold out.

Still, Cohen must not have felt satisfied, because he turned his attention almost exclusively to writing short stories. Perhaps he hoped that stories would allow him the intricacy and character development precluded by his stark poetic scenes. Perhaps he saw the move as a normal step in the evolution of a writer, from brief poems to short stories to the ultimate form of serious literature, the novel. Or maybe he was just trying his hand at different genres. Whatever the case, his stories provide clues into a mind in a state of unrest.

Take, for example, "Saint Jig." Written sometime in 1956 and never published, the story begins by introducing two friends. One, Henry, is charming and confident, the sort of chap who women never resist. His roommate, Jig, is a virgin. He is bright and brooding and immensely appealing, but one of his hands is slightly deformed and he is too self-aware of his disability to attempt courtship. Pitying his friend, Henry proposes he visit a prostitute; it is, he tells Jig, how he himself had become a man. Jig refuses. Paying for sex strikes him as a revolt against the higher order of love. Henry, unmoved, goes to a local brothel and engages the services of one of the women, Ramona. Installing her in a hotel room, he phones Jig and asks him to come right over. Ramona, Henry tells Jig, is an old friend, in town for the night, and could Jig be a sport and show her a good time? Jig agrees, and Henry, rosy with self-satisfaction, goes home to sleep. He is woken up in the middle of the night by a phone call. It's Jig. Come right down and meet us, he tells Henry deliriously. Ramona and I are getting married. Alarmed, Henry stutters. He tries to convince his friend that he shouldn't commit to the first woman who had let him into her graces. Jig protests; he and Ramona, he tells Henry, hadn't had sex. They spent the night talking. And they were in love.

It's a charming story. Like something by Maupassant, it's a ballet of one-note characters that hinges on a final twist. It would be a lovely piece for a twenty-two-year-old to write, all technical mastery and plot and transition and very little that requires the insight that only comes with experience. But right beneath the surviving copies of the story, in a sturdy cardboard box in the library of the University of Toronto, is its original draft. For a spell, it reads the same: Henry suggests a prostitute;

Jig refuses; Henry ambles down to the brothel. But then the story unfurls differently. Instead of getting down to business, Henry walks over to Ramona and calls her by her name. She asks him if they'd met before.

"Don't you remember me, Ramona?" he asks. "Five years ago. Don't you remember you cried; it was the first time that way for you and you cried."

They walk to the hotel. Henry phones Jig. Then he and Ramona talk. They realize that the night they'd slept together was not only Ramona's first as a prostitute, but also Henry's first altogether. "I remember something else," Ramona says softly. "I remember that you kissed my shoulder and I felt your tears on my skin." Henry is moved. "He wanted to hold her, to caress her, to tell her that he remembered everything, how she looked and spoke and wept those important five years ago, and how everything had changed so irrevocably, for him and for her. He was overwhelmed with nostalgia and passion."

Henry grows anxious and emotional. Ramona grows teary. She tells Henry that she remembers it all very vividly. Nobody, she said, has ever treated her so tenderly since. Henry wants to flee. He knows that Jig is on his way. He doesn't want to hurt his friend. "Listen, Ramona," he says. "Probably neither of us should be here right now. It's not a good idea to go back in time, to relive what is already past. Nothing is going to be changed anyway. We are what we are, and no second chances. A lot of people want to be different than they are." But Ramona hears nothing. "She was remembering herself as a young girl," Cohen wrote, "weeping with a young boy, the whole world ahead of them."

And then Jig arrives. "He opened the door very quietly and

what he saw in the lighted room was two naked bodies, limbs enmeshed, moving. He recognized one of the bodies as Henry's, shut the door silently and fled. Back in the dormitory he shoved all his belongings into a large suitcase and ran down the stairs into the street, too hurt to cry."[16]

It's a bit of a wobbly ending. The whole story is unbalanced, with the first two-thirds emotionally thin, just two guys contemplating girls, before swirling into a crescendo of desire that tears the whole plot apart. Henry and Ramona catch fire; two practitioners of callous sex, they are overwhelmed by intimacy. And Jig—who, in the final draft, is a hapless and unscathed lover—is sacrificed, robbed of his innocence and his friendship with Henry by a desire too violent to be contained. Despite the imperfections, comparing the two versions tells us a lot about the author's state of mind. Cohen got it right the first time. He wrote a story that is simultaneously sad and sexy, less an account of a youthful fling than an allegory for love's internal complications. It's throbbing with feeling. Like Henry and Ramona's relationship, the story is sudden, senseless, and sultry—which, if you're lucky, is what life is like in your twenties. But having hit his stride and captured all this turmoil, Cohen wanted out. He toned down his prose, tamed his wild creations. He replaced the vicious ending with a clever joke, and he typed the final draft neatly in three copies and kept them in his drawer. He didn't want to be the kind of writer who observed the ways in which men and women who set out to love each other ended up ravaging each other instead. At least not for a while. Instead he wrote more stories, nearly all of which resemble the final version of "Saint Jig" in their bloodless adherence to easy plot turns and small, self-contained scenes.

Many of these featured a character named Mr. Euemer, an emotionally paralyzed man who feels anything only when he succumbs to the surreally wrought cruelties of those surrounding him. In one story Euemer obeys his wife's demands and shaves his entire body. In another he becomes entangled with a psychopathic youth. Misunderstandings and role reversals abound. Nothing is ever terribly touching or raw.

Cohen's journal from the same period, however, is a very different story. Here he needed no religious imagery or plot devices. He wrote bluntly about what he did and what he felt, about his aimless nocturnal walks down to the novelty shops and the strip clubs of St. Catherine Street, about what went through his mind, about life in his mother's house:

> Sometimes when I got home my mother would be on the telephone describing my coat to the police. As I prepared for bed she'd rage outside my closed door demanding explanations, reciting the names of children who brought their parents pleasure and honour, calling on my dead father to witness my delinquency, calling on God to witness her ordeal in having to be both a father and a mother to me. I would fall asleep in the torrent thinking usually of the exhausted school-day that awaited me.
>
> I don't know what it was that drove me downtown two or three nights a week. There were often long dark blocks between the windows I loved. Walking them, hungry for the next array, I had a heroic vision of myself: I was a man in the middle-twenties, rain-coated, battered hat pulled low above intense eyes, a history of injustice in

his heart, a face too noble for revenge, walking the night along some wet boulevard, followed by the sympathy of countless audiences.

My creation was derived from the lonely investigations of private eyes into radio or movie crimes, family accounts of racial wandering, Bible glories of wilderness saints and hermits. My creation walked with the trace of a smile on his Captain Marvel lips, he was a master of violence but he dealt only in peace. He knew twenty languages, all the Chinese dialects, hardly anyone had ever heard him speak. Loved by two or three beautiful women who could never have him, he was so dedicated, every child who ever saw him loved him. He wrote brilliant difficult books and famous professors sometimes recognized him in streetcars but he turns away and gets off at the next stop.

If we could ever tell it, how it happens, we grow to approximate the vision (minus the nobility, trace of smile, languages, mastery), we get what we wanted, we grow in some way towards the thirteen-year-old's dream, training ourselves with sad movies, poems of loss, minor chords of the guitar, folk-songs of doomed socialist brotherhood. And soon we are strolling the streets in a brand-new trench coat, hair in careful disarray, embracing the moonlight, all the pity of the darkness in a precious kind of response to the claim of the vision, but then much later, when we are tired of indulgence and despise the attitude, we find ourselves walking the streets in earnest, in real rain, and we circle the city almost to morning until we know every wrought-iron gate, every old mansion, every mountain view. In these compulsive journeys we become dimly aware of a new vision, we pray that it might be encouraged to grow and take possession, overwhelm the old one, a vision of order, austerity, work and sunlight.[17]

Melancholia, wanderlust, delusions of grandeur: they were too much to take. Cohen tried several remedies. He spent a semester in law school. He spent some months working for his uncles. He drove down to New York, rented an apartment on Riverside Drive, and enrolled at Columbia, studying English and writing more stories. But none of these felt right; the routines of work or of graduate school could not curb his desires or his sense that there was a better way of being that he simply hadn't discovered yet. Frustrated, he wrote a maniacal short novel, *Ballet of Lepers*. In it a young man much like himself is forced to take in his grandfather, a sweet but fierce man much like Cohen's own, the rabbi Klinitsky-Klein. The grandfather is losing his mind, and punctuates his interactions with short bursts of violence. If a window refuses to open, he smashes it. If a clerk provides poor service, he socks him. Slowly the grandson is entranced, understanding that the old man is not just a lunatic but some sort of a strong-armed Bartleby: Like Melville's scribe, he'd rather not succumb to the degradations of modern, commercial life. Instead of inaction, he opts for a jab or a punch. Soon, the young man follows suit, directing his rage at one poor lowly official. If Cohen had ever sent the manuscript to publishers—by most accounts, he had—it is clear why it was rejected. It's a gorgeous work, but it's too dense with grotesque moments, and too faithful to its own feverish rhythms, to make much sense to the casual reader. With his drawers now bursting with middling manuscripts, Cohen was back to the same question that had been haunting him since he first found Lorca: how to be a poet in a world that increasingly expected its poets either to act up on television or languish in obscurity.

His answer was simple but inspired. He would blend truth and artifice until his audiences didn't know which was which. He would entertain, but deliver the sort of punch lines that carried a real and existential punch. To achieve that he needed a public persona, and so he became the Poet. In the strip clubs and the jazz joints and the oily eateries of St. Catherine Street, Leonard Cohen was reborn as John Keats. At Birdland, a third-floor lounge on top of Dunn's Famous Steak House, he gave midnight readings, sitting on a stool, softly illuminated by a rosy spotlight and accompanied by a six-piece band. He was there to entertain. "I hope there are no atheists here I may offend by this reverence," he would say, introducing his poem "Prayer for Messiah" as the pianist tapped out a prelude by Chopin. He was no less fluid offstage: A friend who had assigned him to review a scholarly book for a student magazine arrived at his place late the night before it was due and found him lounging on the bed, chatting about the I-Ching and the spiritual benefits of masturbation, his piece unwritten.[18]

Such mannerisms weren't merely tolerated, they were adored. These were, after all, the late 1950s, years of white T-shirts and blue jeans and black leather jackets. Strong, rationally argued convictions were suspect. To be hip you had to be a little lost. And Cohen was the first to claim his own aimlessness; his path, he told a television crew following him around in 1964, was infinitely wide and without direction.[19] For the generation that rose between *Howl* and *Sgt. Pepper's Lonely Hearts Club Band*, a touch too young to have dug Ginsberg and Kerouac and just slightly too old to turn on, tune in, and drop out, it was a perfect pace.

Here is what he looked like to the young men, still wearing ties, and the young women, skirts still below the knee, who came to see him perform in the early 1960s. Despite having had two collections of poetry published and the press being fond of calling him the finest poet of his generation, when he took the stage, he was perpetually timid, clasping his book of poems tight to his chest, averting his gaze. His smile was nervous, his voice flat. But then he spoke, and his rhythm was perfect.

"The other time I was in quarters such as these," went one anecdote, "was in the Verdun mental hospital in Montreal. I was visiting"—break for laughter—"visiting a friend. He was on a top floor. And I asked him, for he was still lucid, where can I get a coffee. He said, downstairs. That was one of those famous last words. I commenced a descent of similar stone corridors, and I found myself in a kind of arena, which was surrounded by closed doors. It had been a hot afternoon, and I had removed my jacket, as I am wont to do."—chuckles—"I had left it with my friend, who although mentally ill, was no thief."—rolling laughter—"I suspect he wasn't even mentally ill. He was doing this instead of college."—laughter, applause—"I stood watching the four or five doors, wondering about all the possibilities. Except the one that occurred: door opened, and two large men in white uniforms walked out. And they said, 'where are you supposed to be now?'—nervous giggles—I said, 'in the cafeteria.' They nodded to each other. 'Where are you supposed to be now?' 'In the cafeteria!' Well, you see, as their questions continued, my answers, which started innocent enough, began to sound like I was protesting too much. In fact, after being interrogated three or four more times, I was shouting, pushing them aside, causing them to run after me down the corridor. It was only when a guard identified me that I was able to go back to my friend, who had eaten my jacket."[20]

"Quarters such as these," "as I am wont to do"—that formal language, intricately laid down, all to serve a wisp of a story.

Or perhaps Cohen was smarter. Perhaps he realized that the only way for a young man to talk seriously about religion in a world that seemed too distracted to care for it was to provide more distractions, to tell jokes, to baffle his listeners so profoundly that they lost all sense of place and had to stop and wonder what was going on. Such, at least, was Pierre Berton's reaction: The bow-tied éminence grise of Canadian journalism had Cohen on a panel early on in the poet's career, and had little idea what to do with him. Grave-faced, Berton asked Cohen about his concerns.[21]

"I," Cohen responded, staring at the desk, "I haven't a single concern."

"Come on now," Berton insisted. "What do you care about, really? Don't you care about anything? How can you be a good poet and not care about something?"

That miffed Cohen. "I do the poetry," he quipped at the host, "you do the commentary."

But Berton wasn't letting go. "Let's get this straight," he said calmly, staring at Cohen. "Are you saying that there's nothing that worries you, nothing that bothers you? How can you write poetry if you're not bothered by something?"

Leaning forward, picking up steam as he spoke, Cohen replied. "I'm bothered," he said, "when I get up in the morning, my real concern is to discover whether or not I'm in a state of grace. And I make this investigation, and if I'm not in a state of grace, I try to go to bed."

It's a charming statement, and its vague absurdity helps it linger for a spell longer than a quip usually does. It compels you to imagine what a state of grace might feel like, and why, really, you should bother getting out of bed graceless at all. The sound bite blossoms into a moment of meditation; that's as great a poetic achievement as any carefully wrought stanza.

To the suited adults who paid him around one hundred dollars per television appearance, the Poet was skillfully walking the line between genuine artist and smirking con man. Everybody knew that Leonard Cohen was playing the part of Leonard Cohen, just as Irving Layton played Irving Layton and another young man who was considered a poet down south in New York's Greenwich Village, Robert Allen Zimmerman, was playing the part of Bob Dylan. What was less obvious was that behind all the quips and the jokes, the outrageous performances on TV and the spotlights in seedy clubs, Cohen was never lost in the fun house. Jokes, he realized, and televised spectacles, were the only language his generation spoke fluently. Even if he could fashion himself into a Canadian Lorca, who, in the late 1950s and early 1960s, would want to listen to his sad and soulful tales? What they wanted was for their idols to be cool, and Cohen knew just how to deliver. But his performance pieces were nothing like Layton's. They weren't empty explosions of confidence and style. They were cluster bombs. They dropped fast, penetrated deeply, and set off a series of ongoing explosions that resonated long after they were first heard. In the years of being the Poet, Cohen's aim had grown accurate. What he needed now was a target.

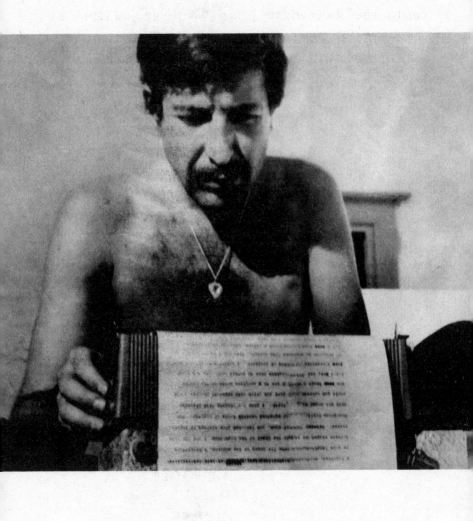

CHAPTER THREE

The Prophet in the Library

I f Leonard Cohen was the Poet, Mordecai Richler was the Novelist. With his first novel published in 1954, two years before Cohen's first poetry collection, Richler was soon celebrated as an important young voice in Canadian letters. He was also, in almost every way, Cohen's opposite. Cohen grew up in affluent Westmount; Richler in the working-class Jewish neighborhood downtown, along St. Urbain Street. Cohen was fascinated by mythology; Richler wrote gruffly about everyday life. Cohen was subtle and elegant; Richler dived right in for the kill. "*Yentas*, flea-carriers and rent-skippers," he wrote of his fellow Jews in one characteristically disdainful paragraph, "*goniffs* from Galicia, couldn't afford a day in the country or tinned fruit for dessert on the High Holidays. They accepted parcels from charity matrons (Outremont bitches) on Passover, and went uninvited to bar-mitzvahs and weddings to carry off cakes, bottles, and chicken legs. Their English was not as good as ours. In fact, they were not yet Canadians."[1]

This tension between divergent attitudes and competing worldviews antedated the two young writers. Hirsch Cohen,

Leonard's great-uncle, and Yudel Rosenberg, Richler's grand-father, had decades earlier been involved in a violent feud: Both were rabbis, both vied for control of Montreal's Jewish community, and both presented radically different approaches to Jewish life. Hirsch Cohen was a measured man who reached out to all members of the community, even those with whose opinions he disagreed, and embraced many of the facets of modern life. Yudel Rosenberg, on the other hand, was a mystic and a scold, fond of reproachful speeches and distrustful of many of his fellow Jews.

Like his grandfather, but for different reasons, Richler looked around him and saw a community largely beyond redemption. Rosenberg was furious because Jews had become too secular and read unholy books; Richler was riled because Jews were not secular enough, retaining something of the ghetto wherever they went. Grandfather and grandson alike, however, addressed their dismay in the same fashion: by look-ing away. Rosenberg transcended the humdrum by turning to the otherworldly realms of the kabbalah, while Richler's escape was more literal—he spent nearly twenty years living in London, making light of his roots. The only way for Jews to overcome their fundamental predicament, Richler believed, was to keep wandering and hope that they would one day go far enough to reach a place where the constraints of their religion could no longer confine them. He felt the same way about being Canadian: The only way to make sense of that identity was to abandon it.

"The best influences in the world reach us from New York," Richler once wrote in a Canadian magazine. "The longest unmanned frontier in the world is an artificial one and I look forward to the day when it will disappear and Canadians will join fully in the American adventure. To say this in Canada is still to invite cat-calls and rotten eggs. We would lose our identity, they say, our independence. But Texas or Maine still have distinctive identities and we are even now economically dependent on the United States."[2]

Leonard Cohen read Richler's article when it first came out in 1964. He was living on the Greek island of Hydra, in a white house on top of a cliff, with a Norwegian woman and her son. The island, he wrote to his sister, had "no tourists except the occasional burning-eyes, badly dressed, miserly, worried looking, pubic bearded individuals who by their expression and dress take pains to advertise the already loosely guarded secret that they are Artists. One hides behind fishermen to avoid them only to find one staring at you in the mirror of your vestibule."[3] And yet, if Cohen himself was a miserly and worried-looking artist, he was very much a *Canadian* miserly and worried-looking artist, and talk welcoming the co-optation of his homeland by the United States felt like betrayal. On a brief visit to Montreal, he told a reporter that if he'd met Richler, "I'd have punched him in the nose."[4]

Violence was merited; Richler had offended not some impotent sense of patriotism but the very foundation of the creative process. "Only nationalism produces art," Cohen stated, denying the common perception that exaggerated patriotism inspired nothing but simplistic, chest-thumping drivel. For him art and nationalism both originated from the same drive, the desire to speak passionately and without restraint about one's origins. "It's only when people start deploring the erosion of their natural resources that they start to worry about their poets."[5] Jingoism, chauvinism, excessive pride—only by tilling the earth with such blunt tools would poetry bloom. Richler's article, Cohen concluded, was an "outright betrayal."[6]

He was speaking at an impromptu press conference at the Museum of Fine Arts. He wore a tight leather jacket and a skinny black tie, and the cigarette dangling from his mouth at a sharp angle made him look less like a person and more like a collection of straight lines that had temporarily coalesced into human form. As was his habit when speaking to the press, every other reply was a quip or a joke. Asked where he was going next, for example, he smiled and replied, "Suicide!"[7] But he wasn't joking when he spoke of Richler and Canada and the arts.

"What it boils down to is that we're frightened of making fools of ourselves politically and artistically. That's exactly what we must do . . . produce with the courage to fail and shed this phony sophistry, this dream of urbanity that isn't ours. I'm tired of this critical attitude that pontificates on what is good and what meets required standards. In this country, we're scared of being labeled hicks, yet no one cares: They don't care in London, they don't care in New York. I don't go along with the sophisticated attitude that ridicules all talk of a new Canadian flag and the rest of the Canadania that we're immersed in each and every day. Unless we explore our own possibilities—these things we consider corny—then we'll lose something valuable."[8]

He wasn't talking only about Canada. By 1964 Leonard Cohen was thirty. The boy poet, Layton's student, the grinning con man—the act was wearing thin. In his hillside home overlooking the Aegean, unfurnished save for a bed and a large wooden table, he spent hours each day writing. There were no jazz clubs in Hydra for him to fill with his poetry, and no one in Greece was particularly impressed by assigning new meanings to old myths. It was the perfect disinterested atmosphere in which Cohen could find his preoccupation, the one theme that, with slight variations, would consume him throughout his career.

That theme was redemption. He had gleaned it from being a Cohen and noting the commanding way in which his clan imposed its will on its surroundings. He was taught it in downtown dances, where he pined after the laughing Catholic French-speaking girls who wanted nothing to do with him and his world. On the wall of one Montreal café he had scrawled one of his finest poems about being saved: "Marita Please Find Me, I Am Almost 30."[9] Redemption was a discretely Jewish affair, a wholly Canadian affliction, an entirely universal obsession. It was more than enough for a lifetime of work. And it wasn't easy to grasp: Cohen's early poems twinkled with moments of sudden clarity, the poet here and there catching a glimpse of his guiding star. But by the time he sat down in the Montreal museum gallery and talked about socking Mordecai Richler, he was well on his way to becoming an artist in full.

To the extent that Cohen owed his clarity to anyone, he was probably indebted to Abraham Moses Klein. Irving Layton may have been the mischievous big brother teaching Cohen how to be in the world as a young poet, but Klein was the elder statesman whose ideas Cohen found too intoxicating to ignore. As a student at McGill in the late 1920s, Klein was attracted to the pride of poets, led by F. R. Scott, who were then trying to infuse the staid local scene with shots of Continental modernism. He soon became one of Canada's most important poets in addition to being a lawyer, a journalist, a leader of the Jewish community, and a speechwriter for Samuel Bronfman, who had made a vast fortune with his Seagram distillery.

For young Canadian Jews, born as Klein began his literary ascent, the poet was a seminal figure. Richler, in his finest novel, *Solomon Gursky Was Here*, reimagines Klein as L. B. Berger, a brilliant writer forced to sell his soul and waste his talent in the service of a whiskey baron. Cohen was far more generous in his assessment. After an unsuccessful run for parliament, Klein's sanity began to flicker. He attempted suicide, was hospitalized, and upon his release spent two decades in self-imposed solitude. Observing Klein's disintegration, Leonard Cohen wrote "To a Teacher," a poem that was included in his second collection, *The Spice-Box of Earth*, published in 1961. "Did you confuse the Messiah in a mirror," Cohen asks Klein, "and rest because he had finally come? / Let me cry Help beside you, Teacher. / I have entered under this dark roof / As fearlessly as an honoured son / Enters his father's house."[10]

Although known mainly as a poet, Klein's most accomplished work was his single novel, *The Second Scroll*. Written in the wake of a trip Klein took to the newly founded state of Israel in 1949, it tells the story of a young Canadian Jew who sets out to find his elusive uncle, Melech, Hebrew for "king." Melech had been a Talmudic prodigy, a scholar so radiant as to earn the nickname the Ilui, "the exalted one." Seeing the town's rabbi murdered by his pogrom-happy Catholic neighbors, the Ilui has a crisis of faith and finds comfort in another religion.

Now called Comrade, he rises through the ranks of the Soviet Communist Party, a renowned authority on the decadence of bourgeois European culture. Then the Nazis invade, and Comrade survives by hiding with a local Catholic family and pretending to serve Christ. When the war ends he finds his way to Rome, makes powerful friends in the Vatican, contemplates conversion, but eventually boards a ship headed to Palestine. His nephew, the novel's narrator, chases him around, always arriving just a few days after Melech has left. The uncle leaves behind a trail of crumbs—long, detailed letters that espouse his worldview. An inspired consideration of the Sistine Chapel is presented in full as an appendix: Sent there by his Catholic friends in the hope that Michelangelo's work would make him succumb to the one true faith, Melech sees each biblical scene as a metaphor for the suffering Christians inflicted on Jews.

In Melech, Klein created a strange messiah. Melech toys with many isms, yet remains fundamentally Jewish. He is never spotted in the flesh, yet the stories he tells—and the stories people tell about him—help his adherents believe that a better, more moral world is possible. The more we read of Uncle Melech's journeys, the more we realize his stories are not meant to reshape history but to replace it altogether. It's a radical idea, but it grows more and more appealing as the novel progresses. Faced with a history so rich with savagery, Jews retreat to fiction and tell themselves that if they believe enough in their stories, the Promised Land will turn from fantasy to fact and the death camps will fade from memory, becoming a distant, grim fable. This is how the Jewish messiah redeems his followers: not by whisking them off to a better world, but by teaching them how to see this one differently.

Some assembly is required—those who want to be saved have to go ahead and, like the novel's narrator, learn how to save themselves—but once the art is mastered, change is imminent. As the Klein scholar Linda Rozmovits elegantly put it, "The Jewish narrator is forced to respond to the alarming paradox that it is in actual fact and not in the recounting of fact that Jewish existence has been rendered most nearly fictional. As the only remaining source of cultural continuity, it falls to the narrator not simply to re-tell but in fact to reconstruct, or to quote one of Klein's favorite puns, to literally 're-member' what has been dismembered."[11]

As a young poet Leonard Cohen was never particularly close to Klein. But when Cohen was invited to give a talk at the Jewish Library in Montreal, a few days after Christmas in 1964, it was Klein he wanted to talk about.

No recording or detailed written account survives of this talk, only a stack of papers—Cohen's own notes. They're disjointed and cryptic, with words sometimes misspelled and sometimes crossed out and sentences trailing off as their author's mind wanders from one budding idea to another. Yet it merits being ranked among Cohen's most notable works, as it marks his transformation from a young seeker of meaning and experimenter with form to a fierce, adult artist who has found his truth and is determined to tell it and tell it again. What came before the speech[12] were good poems, neatly symbolic and pleasantly profound and easy to admire. What came after it was daring work—poems and prose about Hitler and fucking and cruel sacrifice—that baffled critics, repelled many of Cohen's fans, and, eventually, led to his structural transformation from poet to singer. The title of Cohen's speech was "Loneliness and History."[13]

"I am afraid I am going to talk about myself," he began. "All my best friends are Jews but I am the only Jew I know really well." What was to follow, he added, would be a personal statement. "I have been influenced by a remark of Emerson's," he continued. "It is this. What you are, speaks so loudly that I cannot hear you, that is, reality speaks so loudly in you that I can't hear what you are saying. I ask you to apply this insight to me. I shall apply it to you. I will always feel what you are more deeply than what you say."

With that he was ready to introduce the person at the center of his talk. "I remember AM Klein speaking, whose poems disturbed me because at certain moments in them he used the word 'we' instead of the word 'I,' because he spoke with too much responsibility, he was too much a champion of the cause, too much the theorist of the Jewish party line. . . . And sometimes his nostalgia for a warm, rich past becomes more than nostalgia, becomes, rather, an impossible longing, an absolute and ruthless longing for the presence of the divine, for the evidence of holiness. Then he is alone and I believe him. Then there is no room for the 'we' and if I want to join him, if, even, I want to greet him, I must make my own loneliness."

But Klein's loneliness breeds silence, and his silence makes it clear that he has chosen to be a priest. An artist, Cohen said, should become one of two things: a priest or a prophet. Before explaining the differences between the two, he berated the Canadian Jewish community, where honor had migrated "from the scholar to the manufacturer where it hardened into arrogant self defense. Bronze plaques bearing names like Bronfman and Beutel were fastened to modern buildings, replacing humbler buildings established by men who loved books in which there were no plaques at all." This new community had nothing but contempt for the poor and the learned, Cohen said, recalling the dismissive way in which the parents in the affluent neighborhood where he grew up treated their children's teachers, scruffy immigrants with no possessions and the smell of failure. What such a wicked community needed, he argued, was not a priest but a prophet.

But Klein had chosen to become the former. "He became their clown," Cohen continued. "He spoke to men who despised the activity he loved most. He raised money. He chose to be a priest and protect the dead ritual. And now we have his silence." The priest kept the community intact. And the community was "like an old lady whose canary has escaped in a storm, but who continues to furnish the cage with food and water and trapezes in the convinced hope that the canary will come back. The priest tries to persuade her that this optimism is religion."

The prophet knows better. Realizing that history is just the narrative describing the path of "an idea's journey from generation to generation," he continues to chase the idea as it fluctuates, mutates, changes forms, "trying never to mistake the cast off shell with the swift changing thing that shed it." The prophet follows the idea wherever it goes, and ideas, by their very nature, like to travel to dangerous places. The chase, then, is a lonely sport, and the community, observing the prophet, becomes suspicious. Most people would rather visit lifeless and antiquated things in air-conditioned museums than seek thrills in steaming swamps, running the risk of getting bitten by something wild.

"Some moment in time," Cohen said as the speech drew to an end, "very brief, there must have been, among the ancient Hebrews, men who were both prophet and priest in the same office. I tease my imagination when I try to conceive of the energy of that combination. Their lives burned with such an intensity that we here can still feel their warmth. I love the Bible because it honours them." But the two roles had separated, and now artists had a choice to make. Klein stuck with the priesthood. He wrote speeches for the Bronfmans and edited the *Canadian Jewish Chronicle* and ran for office. He, like Cohen's own ancestors, was a guardian of institutions. What he defended was the abstract idea of a Jewish community and its ancient ways. But those ideas were no longer relevant by the time Cohen gave his speech. "I believe we have eliminated all but the most blasphemous ideas of God," he said as he ended his speech. "I believe that the God worshipped in our synagogues is a hideous distortion of a supreme idea—and deserves to be attacked and destroyed. I consider it one of my duties to expose [the] platitude which we have created."

That was a job for the prophet. It was also the path Klein himself had traced so well in *The Second Scroll*. The prophet, like Uncle Melech in the novel, could try on new and conflicting identities and shed them whenever he pleased, because his commitment was not to staid rituals but to a throbbing story. The story had kept the Jews alive. It captivated them even when the somber and accurate accounts of their progressions— thousands burned here, millions gassed there—were too much to bear. Canada, too, was surviving on account of a story: Its own chronology seared by divisions and stained by war, it told itself that it existed, that it was a real nation with a real unifying force, and, encouraged by that story, it persevered. While all nations are, to some extent, imagined communities that come together only when all of their inhabitants envision them into being, Canadians and Jews had to imagine harder, hard enough to override history's long odds.[14]

That is what so infuriated Cohen about Richler's flippant comments: The moment you believed that it would be better to blur the border and join the United States, you'd brought the Canadian story to an abrupt end. The moment you argued that the Jews surrounding you were just too repellent with their customs and their tongue—that one was better off running away to where they couldn't be found—you'd closed the book on Jewish life. Do that, and the world becomes nothing more than a collection of disinterested and disconnected facts, an empty space in which individuals float alone, like particles, some surviving and some not. To create order, to make a community, to shape time, to find hope where logic and reason saw none: This is what the story accomplished. It was the prophet's job to tell the story. And speaking to his fellow Montreal Jews, Leonard Cohen declared it his task to take on, although to do it properly, he noted, he would have to go into exile, like Melech, and stay stoic as his fellow Jews labeled him a traitor for daring to think up other possibilities for spiritual life—possibilities, like love and sex and drugs and song, for which there was little room in the synagogue. He was ready.

As he finished his talk, the shouting began. His words about killing God, prophets as traitors, and the soulless rich enraged many in the audience. Some catcalled. Others demanded the time to debate. It was late at night, and the event's organizers suggested that the discussion be continued the following Saturday night. Grumbling, irate, the audience scattered. The following Saturday the library was packed once again. On the dais, rabbis and community leaders sat gravely, ready to chastise Cohen for his impudence. But Cohen was gone.

CHAPTER FOUR

Notes from a Greek Isle

He was on Hydra. He had bought the house on the hill several years before, cobbling together royalties, literary prize money, and a small family inheritance. How he ended up in Greece is the subject of another one of Cohen's favorite stories—this one, too, possibly apocryphal. It was the winter of 1960, and Cohen, then the author of two collections of poetry, several short stories, and one rejected novel, decided to leave Montreal and travel to recharge his creative drive. London was an obvious choice for a young man raised by Anglophiles who wore British tweeds and looked to the motherland as the source of all that was proper. It was also a place where a young poet could try to connect with the ghosts of Byron and Shelley and Blake. He lived with friends, bought an Olivetti typewriter, and worked for hours each day on his poetry as well as on what was shaping up to be a quasi-autobiographical novel comprising scenes depicting the adolescence of a clever and lost Montreal Jew named Breavman. One day, while strolling around London's East End, he spotted a branch of the Bank of Greece. The weather was London dreary, colorless and soggy, but inside the bank, behind the counter, stood a tanned man wearing shades. Cohen could not resist his siren song—"It was," he told an interviewer some years later, "the most eloquent protest against the landscape that I've seen"[1]—and walked inside. A quick conversation revealed that the man was himself Greek, and he and Cohen began chatting about the weather. In Greece, the tanned man said, it was always springtime. The next day Cohen was Athens-bound.

Whether or not the story of how he got there is true, once installed on the shores of the Aegean, Cohen was ready to begin his exile in earnest. Every now and then, when his finances permitted—the Hydra years are dotted with frequent letters to friends, relatives, and publishers, stressing Cohen's lack of funds and asking for advances or loans—he returned to Montreal for a short spell, to "renew my neurotic affiliations."[2] The rest of the time he was on Hydra, drinking at Katsikas's taverna or sitting on top of the whitewashed well just outside Douskas's taverna, singing and strumming on his guitar. The men and women with whom he spent his days belonged to the same class of itinerant artists; they were writers and painters and filmmakers from the United States, England, Australia, and elsewhere, sensitive enough to resent the humdrum of popular culture and affluent enough to hide from it on some beach. On Hydra they found the sort of virginal beauty that they hoped would facilitate their immaculate rebirth. The island looked the part: Approached by boat, it juts out of the sea like a pyramid, its houses tumbling into the blue bay. In 1962, when the director Jules Dassin, another wandering Jew, retold *Phaedra* with Melina Mercouri and Anthony Perkins as the cursed lovers, he set it on Hydra; the movie's strong eroticism owes as much to its caressing shots of sun-splattered shores and lush gardens as it does to the two characters whose indiscretion it depicts.

Two months after his arrival, Cohen was tangled in an affair of his own, with Marianne Ihlen, the twenty-five-year-old girlfriend of the Norwegian writer Axel Jensen. Jensen took the boat back to Athens shortly after the birth of their son, also named Axel, met another woman, and slowly faded from Ihlen's life. Cohen had seen the family ambling on the island before, but never approached them. After Axel had decamped and left Marianne alone, he sought an introduction. "I was standing in the shop with my basket waiting to pick up bottled water and milk," Ihlen recalled years later. "And he is standing in the doorway with the sun behind him. And then you don't see the face, you just see the contours. And so I hear his voice, saying: 'Would you like to join us, we're sitting outside?' And I reply thank you, and I finish my shopping. Then I go outside. And I sit down at this table where there were three or four people sitting, who lived in Hydra at the time. He was wearing khaki trousers, which were a shade more green. And also he had his beloved, what we in the old days called tennis shoes. And he also always wore shirts with rolled up sleeves. In addition he had a beautiful little sixpence cap. What I didn't know when I met him was that he knew everything about what had happened before I returned. Because after all he had been there, and realized what was going on. So I think that already when he saw me he had enormous compassion for me and my child. But I remember well that when my eyes met his eyes I felt it throughout my body. You know what that is. It is utterly incredible."[3] Eventually Ihlen said her good-bye and sweated as she labored up the hill with her heavy bag of groceries. When she got home, she thought of Leonard. He was immensely attractive, but he also emitted the sort of comforting warmth that reminded her of her grandmother. It was a heady combination. She got up and started to dance.

Before too long Ihlen moved into Cohen's sparsely furnished home. She was afraid that her child would disturb Leonard's work, but was delighted to discover that Cohen had the same calming effect on the boy that he had on her: Each morning, Cohen would call out to Axel, telling him that he needed help in the study. Axel would rush in and, lying on the floor beside Cohen, would draw silently while Cohen wrote. This peaceful routine was dotted with daily strolls down to the beach, lovemaking with Marianne on a cast-iron Russian-made bed, dinners with friends, and the other discrete pleasures of living on an island where the power was often down for all but two hours of the day and you had to bribe the garbage man to pick up your trash.

But if his days on Hydra were tranquil, Cohen's writing was anything but. He was obeying Flaubert's old dictum, which held that a writer ought to be orderly in life so that he may be violent in his work. And violent he was. His poems were no longer the careful juxtaposition of the profane and the sublime. He no longer cared for balance. He was, in the words of one insightful critic, an "author auditioning himself for all the parts in an unwritten play," engaged in a "process of self-recovery and self-discovery."[4] This meant that style and subject matter alike had to be bludgeoned; what still lived after the blows would be the real Leonard Cohen.

Often this process made the poems read more like lists, purely informative and bereft of artifice. In the poem "All There

Is to Know About Adolph Eichmann," for example, Cohen provides a mundane list of attributes, the sort usually associated with a passport or a driver's license—"EYES: Medium / HAIR: Medium," and so on—before concluding with acerbic observations, casually delivered: "What did you expect? / Talons? / Oversize incisors? / Green saliva? / Madness?" Decades later critics labeled Cohen's work from this period as postmodern. But, unlike his postmodern contemporaries, Cohen was never particularly interested in form as such and did not set out to deconstruct poetry. He was trying to touch the rawest synapses of the Jewish and Western psyches. Written in 1963, Cohen's poem must have been influenced by Eichmann's trial, taking place that year in Jerusalem. Although he doesn't mention her by name, Cohen sides with Hannah Arendt, who, covering the trial for *The New Yorker*, advanced the theory of the banality of evil. There was nothing particularly rotten about Eichmann, Arendt wrote; he was not a psychopath but merely a painfully average man who regarded the state-sponsored madness around him as normal and therefore never hesitated to partake in its crimes.

To most American intellectuals, many of them Jews, Arendt's essay slid dangerously close to an absolution of the perpetrator, and her tone conveyed a cold disgust for the meek Jews testifying against Eichmann and the prosecutors promoting their case. "What struck one in reading *Eichmann in Jerusalem*—struck like a blow—was the surging contempt with which she treated almost everyone and everything connected with the trial, the supreme assurance of the intellectual looking down upon those coarse Israelis," wrote Irving Howe. "Many of us were still reeling from the delayed impact of the Holocaust.

The more we tried to think about it, the less could we make of it. Now we were being told by the brilliant Hannah Arendt that Adolf Eichmann, far from being the 'moral monster' the Israeli prosecutor had called him, should really be seen as a tiresome, boring, trivial little fellow, the merest passive cog in the machine."[5] Others were less measured in their criticism of Arendt, causing Arendt's friend Mary McCarthy to write: "This Eichmann business is assuming the proportions of a pogrom."[6]

The pogrom was in full force in 1963, and Cohen had chosen to enter it on Arendt's side, even if he didn't share her odd distaste for the victims. He was preoccupied with the Holocaust. When his collection of poems was finally published—in 1964, under the provocative title *Flowers for Hitler*—he prefaced it with the following quotation from Primo Levi: If from the inside of the concentration camp, Levi, a survivor, wrote, "a message could have seeped out to free men, it would have been this: Take care not to suffer in your own homes what is inflicted on us here."[7] The capacity for evil was dormant in us all; if we wished to purge it, we needed to learn how to speak about it first.

Increasingly—and tellingly for a poet about to become a singer and a songwriter—Cohen's way of speaking in verse hardened into rhyming couplets. The imagery of his previous two collections—intricate and soft—was now replaced by lines like these: "History is a needle / for putting men to sleep / anointed with the poison / of all they want to keep."[8] It was the same neat trick he'd learned on the stages of clubs and auditoriums in Montreal, disguising painful truths as aperçus; but as his explorations got deeper and darker, his lines grew more stunning, feeling simultaneously immediately familiar and profoundly incomprehensible—and less personal. *Flowers for Hitler* is densely populated with fathers and grandfathers and family members, none of them Cohen's recognizable kin, all of them stand-ins for the coarse and callous members of the Jewish community that he had come to loathe. If a father appeared in *Let Us Compare Mythologies*, he was, with a few embellishments, Nathan Cohen, and was addressed warmly and elegiacally; in *Flowers for Hitler* there are fathers building the ovens in which millions perish, and others who fill their homes with twisted fears. They are there to be exorcised, leaving their sons "free as a storm-severed bridge, useless and pure as drowned alarm clocks."[9]

But Cohen wasn't just the oedipal tinkerer some of his critics accused him of being. He was exploring these family dynamics not to make a personal point, or to explore the machinations of psychology, but rather to comment, for the first time in his career, on politics. Most of the failed fathers in the book are catalysts of grand disasters: There are direct references and allusions to Aleksandr Kerensky, the Russian prime minister ousted by the October Revolution, and to Joseph Goebbels, captured at the moment when he decides to abandon his career as a writer and join the Nazi Party. Both are weak men, misguided by their passions, unable to stop history's march of folly. They invite nothing from the younger generation—their figurative sons—but pity. And pity Cohen has in spades. He is empathetic in part because he believes, like Arendt, that there's no inherent evil in the world, just thoughtless men in precarious circumstances. In one poem, "Hitler the Brain-Mole"—Cohen had originally wanted to give his collection that title—he notes, "Hitler the brain-mole looks out of my eyes / Goering boils ingots of gold in my bowels / My Adam's Apple bulges with the whole head of Goebbels / no use to tell a man he's a Jew."[10] It's with that insight in mind, Cohen argues, that we should approach world events: Rather than exert our energy taking sides, we should observe carefully until we see that history doesn't sweep but saunter, and that the men who make it occupy more than the single dimension we assign them in our limited imaginations.

This insight had led Cohen to do more than write harsh poems. He wanted to see the broken world for himself. In March 1961 he traveled to Havana. Just before leaving, he wrote a friend back home that he was "wild for all kinds of violence."[11] He was only half joking. Castro had been in power for two years, and Cuba seemed as close as Cohen would ever come to Lorca's bloody and idealistic Spain. Also, Lorca had lived in Cuba for two months in 1930, written about it enthusiastically, and left enough of an impression to have Havana's grandest theater named after him.

But Lorca's Cuba was long gone, and the island Cohen found was a faded rock. All the glamorous, raucous pleasures of Fulgencio Batista's regime—the casinos, the brothels—had been outlawed. Instead of Hemingways the bars were now occupied by mirthless Russian engineers sent by Moscow to supervise its Caribbean satellite. Cohen didn't mind too much.[12] He wore khaki shorts and grew a beard and, ambling around town, soon discovered that the prostitutes and the gamblers were not really gone; too vital to the island's economy, they were merely made less conspicuous, and were all too happy to embrace, as Cohen referred to himself in a later poem, "the only tourist in Havana."

One night a man in a dark suit knocked on Cohen's hotel room door. He identified himself as a Canadian official, and asked Cohen to accompany him to the Canadian embassy at once. There he was rushed into the office of the vice-consul. "Your mother," the diplomat said disdainfully, "is very worried about you."[13] Soon Cohen learned that three B-26 bombers, painted to look like Cuban planes, had taken off earlier that evening from Nicaragua. Supplied by the CIA and piloted by anti-Castro Cuban exiles, the bombers destroyed several of the regime's grounded aircraft near Havana and Santiago. An American invasion seemed imminent, and Mrs. Cohen anxiously called her cousin, a Canadian senator, and asked him to track down her wayward son.

At first Cohen laughed the whole thing off. Two days later, on April 17, Operation Falcon was launched, and nearly fifteen hundred men landed at the Bay of Pigs. Cuba was under attack, and Cohen, a bearded foreigner, was eminently suspicious. He was walking on the beach at Playa de Varadero one day when twelve soldiers with machine guns encircled him. They thought he was one of the invaders. As they walked him to the police station, he repeated, in Spanish, the most comforting sentence he could think of to convince the soldiers he wasn't Kennedy's spy. "Amistad del pueblo," he said repeatedly, "friendship of the people."[14] It did little to convince the soldiers, but before too long Cohen, stringing together a few sentences in Spanish, turned on the same effortless charm he had shown reading poems in public in Montreal. The soldiers poured him a glass of rum, gave him a shell necklace and a piece of string with two bullets to wear as an amulet, hugged him tight, and let him go.

The few American communists he met on the island were less kind. To them he was a "bourgeois individualist."[15] To show his contempt, Cohen met the communists the following day, clean shaven and wearing a seersucker suit. He kept the same amused air when writing to his publisher in Toronto, Jack McClelland, who was about to publish his second collection of poetry, *The Spice-Box of Earth*. "Just think how well the book would sell if I'm hit in an air-raid," he wrote. "What great publicity! Don't tell me you haven't been considering it." Then he delivered a matter-of-fact report on the invasion: "There was a prolonged round of anti-aircraft fire tonight. An unidentified (but we know Yankee) plane. I think the guns were in the room next door. I looked out the window. Half a platoon running down the Prado, then crouching behind an iron lion. Hopelessly Hollywood."[16]

With the invasion's catastrophic end came many arrests, some of them targeting tourists. Cohen decided to leave. So did many of Cuba's wealthier residents, terrified by Castro's renewed zeal. Every day throngs swamped the shelled airport in search of a visa. Cohen joined them, and, eventually, on April 26, managed to secure a ticket out of Havana. But when he lined up to board the plane, the clerk called the person before him, and the person after him, leaving Cohen stranded. Glancing at the passenger list, Cohen saw that his name had been crossed off. He was taken aside by an officer and told he couldn't leave. The reason given was a photograph found in his bag, featuring him, khaki shorts and stubble, hugging the soldiers who had arrested him a few days earlier. It was just too suspicious. He was clearly a troublemaker, not a Canadian poet. He was placed in detention and guarded by a fourteen-year-old with a gun. When a scuffle elsewhere in the airport distracted the armed youth, Cohen got up, left the room, boarded the plane, and told himself everything was going to be all right. A short while later he landed in Miami.

It was in Havana that he wrote the poem about Eichmann, and much of *Flowers for Hitler* soon followed. He had seen power corrupt. "Power chops up frightened men," he wrote to Corlies Smith, his editor at Viking Press in New York. "I saw it in Cuba."[17] And having seen it, he wanted to write about it with the urgency of an Isaiah.

To much of the rest of the world, however, he was a dilettante, hopping from his Greek island to Havana to play at revolution. After the 1962 Cuban missile crisis, he wrote a lighthearted letter to his sister, Esther, poking fun at much of the Cold War's hyperbole and paranoia.[18] Soon her husband wrote back, accusing Cohen of being a pseudointellectual who wasn't morally serious enough to grasp that the conflict pitted good versus evil. Cohen, usually sanguine in his letters, replied harshly, and his reply ran more than seven pages of block text.

"Listen very carefully, Victor," he writes.[19] "I'm no intellectual at all, not pseudo, not neo, not proto, and not even real. Having written at least three respectable books (published) I might be justified in claiming the title, but I'm not even reaching. But I happen to know a fair amount about Cuba, having read almost everything there is on it, and having gone to see it in the raw, with some risks to my person which I haven't ever mentioned to anyone." He goes on to describe his brush with Castro's soldiers, his detention at the airport, and his opposition to "all forms of collectivization, censorship, or control, whether it happens to be on behalf of the enslaved proletariat or the holy values of the free world." His tone heats up: "Don't heave slogans at me. I'm one of the few men of my generation who cared enough about the Cuban reality to go and see it, alone, uninvited, very hungry when my money ran out, and absolutely unwilling to take a sandwich from a government which was shooting political prisoners. So if I sound off a little cynically and flippantly in a letter to my sister, let's put it down to fun and not to ignorance." Then the tone shifts once again, and Cohen, long before his speech at the Jewish Library in Montreal, evokes his prophetic theme. "If I am not mistaken," he writes, "the dramas we are moved to applaud are those in which the prophet resists priestly organization, the man of peace resists the king, the philosopher resists the dogmatists, the scientist resists the theorists, and in general, the wild, obsessed, inspired, gifted, talented individual resists everything that is smug, comfortable or respectable. I invite you to switch sides."

It would have been a fine point on which to end the letter. But Cohen had another page in him. He didn't want to end on a general note. He wanted to be concrete. He wanted to talk politics. Noting that Victor had started his letter referring to the U.S. government as "the greatest going government on earth today" and ended up admitting it was merely a preferable shade of gray in a world in which there were no blacks and whites, Cohen launched into a study of morality in monochrome:

> The cotton-jobbers, politicians, ad-men, generals of
> Charcoal Grey easily become the distribution experts,
> commissars, propagandists, generals of Oxford Grey. It is

only my profession that risks annihilation, and perhaps, the health of my profession really defines the difference between societies. The America I choose is not your grey America, which, at most levels of safe living, is very close to their grey Russia. The America I choose is not the one you hold up to me, to be adored because it does not "persecute" me, restrict my movement, or starve me. Forgive me, if, bred on Whitman, Thoreau, and Emerson, I choose a different America. The truth is, Victor, that war was declared a long time ago, is being fought today on both sides of the Curtain, and its outcome is more important than the temporary and perhaps fictitious struggle between east and west (fictitious not in the sense that it doesn't exist but that there is no real conflict of *values*). It is the war between those who conceive of existence as a dynamic rainbow, and those who conceive of it as a grey monotone; between those who are willing to acknowledge the endless possibilities, agonies, delights, mysteries and destinies of the human predicament, and those who meet every human question with a rigid set of answers, some immutable inheritance from a father or a god or a revolution. This is the old war, Athens against Sparta, Socrates against Athens, Isaiah against the priests, the war that deeply involves "our western civilization," the one to which I am committed.[20]

Cohen had identified his war. But how to fight it? His poems were one way, but increasingly they seemed unfit for the task. He would publish another attempt at unaffected poetry, *Parasites of Heaven*, in 1966, a slim volume whose greatest—and only—shining moments would soon be set to music and made famous as songs. This new style of poetry must not have appealed, because in 1972 he made his views on poetry perfectly clear: Each poem in his newly published collection, *The Energy of Slaves*, had a small illustration of a razor blade printed at the top of the page, announcing that the author was in a cutting mood. "The poems don't love us anymore," he wrote in the volume's most striking poem, "they don't want to love us / they don't want to be poems / Do not summon us, they say / we can't help you any longer." Rather than remain on the page, the poems "have gone back into the world / to be with the ones / who labour with their total bodies / who have no plans for the world / They never were entertainers."[21] After that, Cohen wrote poetry very sporadically, and, when he did, took care to do it violence. When, in 1978, he published *Death of a Lady's Man*, he coupled each poem with a commentary bearing the same title, the effect being that verse and criticism canceled each other out. The two remaining collections of new poetry he would publish in his career—1984's *Book of Mercy* and 2006's *Book of Longing*—continued this trajectory of experimentation, the first consisting mainly of modern-day psalms, and the second of line drawings and erotic musings. The poet has abandoned poetry.

Why? Cohen leaves only a few clues, one of which is a song. In "A Singer Must Die," a track on his 1974 album, *New Skin for the Old Ceremony*, he captures the ordeal shared by the singer and the poet alike:

Now the courtroom is quiet, but who will confess.
Is it true you betrayed us? The answer is yes.

Then read me the list of the crimes that are mine,
I will ask for the mercy that you love to decline.
And all the ladies go moist, and the judge has no choice,
A singer must die for the lie in his voice.
And I thank you, I thank you for doing your duty,
You keepers of truth, you guardians of beauty.
Your vision is right, my vision is wrong,
I'm sorry for smudging the air with my song.

Cohen wasn't being melodramatic; he was being Greek. In his letter to Victor Cohen, just after declaring his commitment to Western civilization, Cohen called on one of its founding fathers, Plato, and quoted a bit from the *Apology*, in which Socrates admits that his fellow Athenians' decision to put him to death doesn't surprise him in the least. But the convictions he explored in *Flowers for Hitler*, heightened in *The Energy of Slaves*, and stated with abundant clarity in *New Skin for the Old Ceremony* come from another Platonic classic, *The Republic*. In the final book of his great epic, the philosopher, having devoted most of his attention to questions of government, takes on an unexpected topic: poetry.

"Speaking in confidence," thunders his Socrates, "I do not mind saying to you, that all poetical imitations are ruinous to the understanding of the hearers, and that the knowledge of their true nature is the only antidote to them."[22] Their true nature, Socrates explains further, is that of the deceiver: The poet doesn't see reality as it is—only the philosophers have that distinction. What he describes in his poems, then, is not truth but appearance, and, being a poet, he applies a host of tricks—clever words, pretty sounds—to make this appearance more appealing than it really is. Any poet, then, is a liar twice over, and a danger-ous one at that: Poetry is calculated to move us, and the only direction in which it can move us is further away from the truth. Not even Homer is spared; the writer of *The Iliad*, Plato warns us, excites our senses, and in our impassioned state we fail to see that he is hazardous to us because he fails to give us what we really need. And what we really need is com-plex. Plato, as the classicist Eric Havelock noted, "expected poetry to perform all those functions which we relegate on the one hand to religious instruction or moral training and on the other to classroom texts, to histories and handbooks, to encyclopedias and reference manuals."[23] Plato, in other words, wanted poetry to bridge the heavenly world—where everything known to man exists in perfect form—and our world, which is imperfect and marred by so many distrac-tions. Lorca could have defined his *duende* just the same, an attempt at capturing a deep truth not immediately evident, an effort at calling on knowledge and feeling to unite and inform us as no other form of education can. But unlike Lorca, Plato believed that poetry was too artificial to deliver on the promise. And Leonard Cohen agreed. The more he understood what he wanted to say—all that prophetic stuff—the less enamored he was of poetry. He needed to find other means of expression.

Novels were one logical detour. Having written the ill-fated *Ballet of Lepers*, he resolved to try again. Originally called *Beauty at Close Quarters*, written mostly in his early years in Hydra, the novel struck many people as wrong for all sorts of reasons. Jack McClelland, who enthusiastically published

Cohen's poetry, thought it was too autobiographical and too steamy, its crude concentration of carnal matters a sure put-off for the decent Canadian reader. The folks at Viking Press liked it, but wanted Cohen to cut it by half. He did, revising as he went along and producing, eventually, a wholly new novel, now entitled *The Favorite Game*, which was published in 1963.

There's much of Leonard Cohen in Lawrence Breavman, the book's protagonist. He's in his late teens and Jewish and fond of leaving his home in Westmount—he lives with his mother, his father having died when he was a boy—and taking long walks to downtown Montreal. He is short, and puts tissues in his shoes to appear taller, which Cohen did as well. He is an enthusiastic hypnotist, and uses his skill to charm the pants off the young maid. The book is told in short anecdotal bursts, which are propelled forward mostly by conversations between Breavman and his best friend, Krantz—modeled after Morton Rosengarten, Cohen's childhood pal—followed by the narrator's own observations, which place their youthful bravado in some world-historical context. Like this:

"Krantz, is it true that we are Jewish?"
"So it has been rumored, Breavman."
"Do you feel Jewish, Krantz?"
"Thoroughly."
"Do your teeth feel Jewish?"
"Especially my teeth, to say nothing of my left ball."
"We really shouldn't joke, what we were just saying reminds me of pictures from the camps."
"True."

Weren't they supposed to be a holy people consecrated to purity, service, spiritual honesty? Weren't they a nation set apart?[24]

The boys in the book talk the way smart and insecure boys talk, an elaborate verbal ritual designed to conceal their voluminous anxiety with a thin layer of icy wit. And the narrator made sure we knew they were not just shooting the breeze; the conversation they were having was the central conversation of Jewish theology, one that began millennia ago and will not end anytime soon. Krantz and Breavman's rendition may have been a touch more profane, but their souls were reaching heavenward. Like every Jew since Abraham, they, too, were baffled by the idea of having been chosen by God, and were trying to figure out just what that meant. And when they weren't thinking about God, they were out to find girls.

Most critics liked the novel, albeit with some reservations. The London *Daily Telegraph* captured the collective enthusiasm by declaring *The Favorite Game* "an odd, off-beat book, with a great deal of muted poetry and some beautifully observed scenes."[25] The *Guardian* called it "a lyrical and exploratory bit of semi-biography."[26]

But Cohen, while grateful for the praise, saw it as nothing of the kind. He shared his frustrations with Layton. "Irving," he wrote, "will you understand, will you understand what no one else will understand, that *The Favorite Game* is a third novel disguised as a first novel? Will you see it as a great detective story in which a body is lost in every paragraph?"[27]

He wasn't joking, or at least not entirely. He didn't set out to write an odd and beautiful and poetic bildungsroman.

He wanted to write about what it was like to be young and try to take flight and realize that life was a terrain made of many plains and very few mountaintops. He wanted to write about small pleasures and big struggles, and to tell other young men and women like him that they needn't look for transcendence because there was so much beauty right here, in dirty streets and dirty talk. He wanted, in other words, to write a very intimate epic. "That's what I always missed when I heard my first fairy-tales—the small talk of giants," he wrote to Layton. "I longed to hear how they lived away from crises. I hated it when they came tumbling down and left the world to the sneaky Davids, the loop-hole artists, the lawyers. Why are the giants always asleep in one part of the story? Because their real enemy was boredom, interior despair, and the worst temptation: a landscape into which they could fit, that is, a world they did not dwarf, that overwhelmed them and limited their freedom. Giants cannot take their landscape seriously, so they fall before clever Jack, Sammy-on-the-run, the bright ambitious son of simple people, who settles with his stolen treasures into the safe life, who bores and trains his grandchildren with the tale of how he tricked a sleeping God. I meet them all and read their manuscripts on their palms. Their successes are not important and their failures are not moving or instructive."[28]

Even though many of the reviewers were enthusiastic, none seemed to get what the book was about. It was the same predicament he'd experienced as a poet: He was lauded for writing well, but forced to play the part of the smooth young prodigy, stripped of nuance, easily explained. Praise held little appeal for Cohen; he was seeking comprehension, and was delighted when, on rare occasions, it appeared. Kenneth N. Cameron, for example, a leading expert on Shelley, wrote Cohen an insightful note, saying that the novel's "episodic appearance is deceptive," and that his work, unlike the more unstructured works by the Beats, had movement, "a total flow which is subtle but strong." Cohen was so thrilled with Cameron's note that he went on to retype almost all of it in a later letter to his sister. "My impression of the book," Cameron wrote, "is that it is very beautiful, very moving and, in spite of some roaringly comic scenes, a very sad book. It is full of a kind of drifting pain that at times is almost unbearable; and it must have been so to you in writing it."[29]

Whether or not it had been, Cohen didn't let on in his notes or his correspondence. But he soon began work on a second novel, and, as he had done before with his verse, was ready to abandon the comforts of a well-received style and reach for deeper truths.

Beautiful Losers was published in 1966. It is one of those rare novels before which commentary and criticism stand helpless, pedantic, and dumb. If *The Favorite Game* was a subtle but strong current, *Beautiful Losers* was the deluge. To the extent that it was about anything, it was about three friends—one of whom possibly imaginary—and their devotion to Catherine Tekakwitha, a seventeenth-century Algonquian Mohawk who was baptized a Catholic, became a saint, and is remembered for her self-mortification and for maxims like "Take courage, despise the words of those who have no faith."[30] The novel is told from shifting points of view, and its prose is liquid. It reads more like a vision than a story. An erotic vision: "Her breasts were small, somewhat muscular, fruit with fiber," Cohen wrote in one representative passage. "Her freakish nipples make me want to tear up my desk when I remember them, which I do at this very instant, miserable paper memory while my cock soars hopelessly into her mangled coffin, and my arms wave my duties away, even you, Catherine Tekakwitha, whom I court with this confession. Her wondrous nipples were dark as mud and very long when stiffened by desire, over an inch high, wrinkled with wisdom and sucking."[31]

Cohen wasn't juxtaposing nipples and saints for literary effect, as he'd done earlier in his career. He was doing it because he now knew that both were essential components of the world, both vessels of pure emotion, deserving of close study and devotion. And he had no other way of capturing these complications than with the manic stream of language and thought that was his new novel. Comparisons to that other practitioner of the same method weren't long in coming: "James Joyce is not dead," declared the *Boston Globe*. "He is living in Montreal under the name of Cohen."[32] Other reviewers were far less gracious: The *Toronto Globe and Mail* called the novel "verbal masturbation,"[33] *Time* announced it to be a "sluggish stream of concupiscence,"[34] and the influential critic Robert Fulford provided the most memorable judgment when he declared *Beautiful Losers* "the most revolting book ever written in Canada."[35]

Faced with such vitriol, Cohen was defiant. Back from Hydra, he was sitting in a CBC studio in Toronto, talking to the interviewer Adrienne Clarkson, deflecting any attempt at earnestness. Clarkson asked about his mother, and how she had reacted to her son's novel being decried as filth. Cohen answered that for his mother, any mention at all was a triumph.

Clarkson asked about the censor, and whether or not Cohen was worried that his work, like Joyce's, may be deemed too indecent for publication. Cohen responded with a joyful and defiant rebuke of censorship. Clarkson tried again, taking the direct approach, asking Cohen how he felt when he read the criticism.

"I'd feel pretty lousy if I were praised by a lot of the people that have come down pretty heavy on me," he said. Then, true to his theme, he announced that there was a war raging on. Clarkson, confused, asked what he was talking about. "Well," Cohen said coyly, "it's an old, old war and I think I'd join the other side if I tried to describe it too articulately. But I think, you know what I mean, there's a war on, and I like to, if I have to choose sides, which I don't generally like to do, but if I have to, then I'd just as well be defined as I have been by the establishment press."[36]

When Cohen first spoke of the war, and of the sides, and of the struggle for Western civilization—most notably in his letter about Cuba to his brother-in-law—he was furious. Sitting in Clarkson's studio, he was amused. Having spent nearly a decade learning how to be a poet and half a decade unlearning the same thing, having risen up and spiraled down as a novelist in the span of three years, he finally felt he'd found the art form that would allow him to convey his ideas: He would sing. It was more lucrative anyway, and, relying as it did on performance, had a transience to it that neatly matched the main ideas he was trying to convey, ideas that rejected all the glorious tomorrows for one solid today.

"I'd like the stuff I do to have that kind of horizontal imme-diacy, rather than something that is going to be around for a long time," he told Clarkson. "I'm not interested in an insurance plan for my work."[37]

He had meant it: From Toronto Cohen traveled to New York, world capital of horizontal immediacy and seat of the record industry, to take up a room at the Chelsea Hotel and reinvent himself as a writer of songs.

CHAPTER FIVE

"One Big Diary,
Set to Guitar Music"

Leonard Cohen's decision to abandon his modestly successful career as a writer and a poet, at the age of thirty-two, in order to become a singer, is so profoundly strange that attempts to explain it tend to be either banal or fantastic. On the one hand, some of Cohen's biographers have suggested that he picked up a guitar when he realized that entertainers were far more handsomely compensated than poets. It's a plausible premise, but it leaves Cohen in the position of being clueless enough to believe that, as an older man—Elvis, born a few months after Cohen, had already become a star and served in the army and made terrible movies and retired from show business by the time Cohen first announced his musical aspirations—with a nasal voice he could simply march down to Manhattan and become a singing sensation. Cohen was always audacious about his career, but he was never naive; money might have played a part in his decision, but it was very likely not the only, or even the central, one. What made him sing? As is the case with all seminal moments in his life, Cohen, when asked, had a fanciful explanation at the ready.

He was, he told an interviewer a decade later, in Toronto's King Edward Hotel. It was the summer of 1965, and he was sitting on the bed and reading a few new poems out loud to a lady friend. The door to the adjoining room was left ajar, and Cohen and his companion could see the couple next door, naked, making love. They could hear them, too: Amused by the spectacle, Cohen began to sync his words with the couple's moaning and groaning, and was immensely pleased with the result. "I think I'm going to record myself *singing* my poems," he told his companion. "Please don't," she replied.[1]

A much more likely story involves not sex but Dylan. Sometime in 1965 Cohen discovered the young Jewish poet, nearly a decade his junior, and was immensely drawn to Dylan's cryptic, haunting lyrics. In his interview with Adrienne Clarkson, he took the time, apropos of nothing, to cite the line from Dylan's "Mr. Tambourine Man" about fading into one's own parade. By the time he attended a drunken gathering of Canada's poets, one week after New Year's Day of 1966, Dylan was all he wanted to talk about.

The party was held at F. R. Scott's house. It started, at noon, with lunch, progressed with copious drinking, slowed down for dinner, and then rocketed into more drinking and merriment. Layton was there, as were Dudek, Al Purdy, and Ralph Gustafson, the editor of an influential anthology of Canadian poetry. The guests had been summoned by a lyrical invitation, carefully composed by Scott, which playfully worked in the titles of the various literary magazines they had all started. It reflected the evening's purpose—not merely a party, but a celebration of that rarest bird in Canada's cultural skies, a cohesive group of poets influencing and enriching one another.

But Cohen wasn't in the mood for poetry. At some point he took out his guitar and posed a question: "What are these poets doing," he asked, "all writing poetry the way they used to? Do you know who the greatest poet in America is?"

"Who?" asked somebody.

"Bob Dylan!" Cohen declared.

No one in the room had any idea who Dylan was.

"Don't you know?" Cohen cried out. "He's already made a million dollars."

"Then he can't be the greatest poet in the world," somebody else quipped. But Cohen persisted. "Don't you know his records?" he asked. It was established that no one did, and Scott, ever the gracious host, dashed out to a nearby store with the names of four of Dylan's albums. Learning they each cost $6.95, he bought two. When he returned, Cohen said that Dylan's albums contained "very good music, very good poetry. It's the greatest poetry of the century." And then the records were placed on the record player and the poets leaned in to listen to the music of the young man from Hibbing, Minnesota.

They loathed it. The music, Scott later recalled, "began to blare such as never had been heard in these walls before." Purdy, perhaps the nation's most celebrated poet, leaped up in the air as if kicked from behind: "It's an awful bore," he said. "I can't listen to any more of this," and then walked into the kitchen in search of more beer. The others were slightly more polite, but none thought Dylan very good. Cohen, however, was undeterred. He got up and excused himself, saying that an audience awaited him in one of the jazz clubs downtown. He left promising that he'd soon be the new Dylan. No one in the room believed him.[2]

It's not hard to see what may have attracted Cohen to Dylan. Like Cohen, Dylan grew up in a family that was actively involved with its local Jewish community, and with a grandfather who studied the Talmud each afternoon. Both men, when young, attended Zionist summer camps—Cohen's called Mishmar, Dylan's Herzl—and were taken with the Jewish folk songs they learned there; in 1961, performing in Greenwich Village, Dylan parodied one such song, "Hava Nagila," which he claimed jokingly was a strange chant he'd learned in Utah. But, most important, Dylan was on fire. Listening to "With God on Our Side" or "Masters of War," it was easy enough to imagine that if Isaiah had been born in the 1940s, he'd've found his way to the stage at the Gaslight Cafe to sing and preach. Listening to Dylan, Cohen heard the same language he'd heard years before, studying the prophets with his grandfather. Sometimes, the lines came directly from the scriptures: "I and I," for example, a song from Dylan's 1984 album *Infidels* and one of Cohen's favorites, features the line "no man sees my face and lives." It was spoken once before, by God, in the book of Exodus.[3]

Dylan wasn't just citing the ancient tradition; he was continuing it. He understood—by most accounts, subconsciously—something profound about the role prophecy played in Jewish life. The rabbi and theologian Abraham Joshua Heschel described that role well: "In speaking about revelation," he wrote, "the more descriptive the terms, the less adequate is the description. The words in which the prophets attempted to relate their experiences were not photographs but illustrations, not descriptions but songs."[4] Even as Jews replaced their ecstatic modes of worship with other, more cerebral ones, they nevertheless kept singing their messianic songs: In his study of Dylan's Jewishness, Seth Rogovoy identified the singer as a modern-day *badkhn*, or joker, a traditional figure serving as "a pious merrymaker, a chanting moralist, a serious bard who sermonized while he entertained . . . the sensitive seismograph that faithfully recorded the reactions of the common man to the counsels of despair and to the messianic panaceas."[5] Dylan tried to be a *badkhn*-as-poet—"I search the depths of my soul for an answer," he declared in an early college poem, "But there is no answer. / Because there is no question. / And there is no time."[6]—before realizing that bards belonged onstage, walking into a coffeehouse called the Ten O'Clock Scholar, introducing himself not as Robert Zimmerman but as Bob Dylan, and securing his first gig.

By 1966 Leonard Cohen was heading in the same direction. He had played music before—in a high school country-and-western band called the Buckskin Boys, with friends in Montreal, and for Marianne and others on Hydra. But he was always more than a casual strummer: Everything he's ever written, he later told an interviewer—the poems, the short stories, the novels, the songs—was just "one big diary, set to guitar music."[7] It could be, of course, that Cohen the singer was trying retroactively to reshape his past, to explain away his strange transformation by claiming that the musical drive had always lain dormant inside. But there are reasons to believe that he was being sincere. For one thing, he made similar claims in other interviews, an unlikely consistency for a canny subject who is fond of taking liberties when asked about the intricacies of his personal life. But there are other sources that suggest that Cohen might have truly heard a guitar playing softly even as he wrote verse and entertained no notions of performance. Lorca is one: For the Spaniard all arts were equally efficient vessels for *duende*, but some were more equal than others. Trained as a classical pianist, Lorca struck an early friendship with the composer Manuel de Falla, who influenced Lorca to conceive of Spanish folk music as the true manifestation of the soul of the people. "The great artists of the south of Spain," Lorca said in one of his lectures on the *duende*, "whether Gypsy or Flamenco, whether they sing, dance, or play, know that no emotion is possible unless the duende comes. They may be able to fool people into thinking they have duende—authors and painters and literary fashionmongers do so every day— but we have only to pay a little attention and not surrender to indifference in order to discover the fraud and chase away their clumsy artifice."[8]

A student of the Bible, Cohen could find similar convictions closer to home. The ancient Hebrew temple, he surely knew, included, in addition to its classes of priests and holy servants, also a phalanx of musicians, the latter considered instrumental in worshipping the Almighty. Again and again, the book of Psalms—which so appealed to Cohen that he later attempted to write his own version of it—instructs its readers to "sing unto the Lord with thanksgiving; sing praise upon the harp unto our God."[9] It was only a matter of time, then, before a young man who increasingly understood his undertaking as being driven by a spiritual engine found his way to that most potent of all art forms.

The question of what it is about music that sets it apart from other pursuits and grants it its theological resonance has been left, surprisingly, largely unexplored, but those who have considered it offer ideas that go a long way toward explaining Cohen's turn to song. Music, wrote the French economist Jacques Attali, "heralds, for it is *prophetic*. It has always been in its essence a herald of the times to come."[10] Attali carried Lorca's ideas a step further, arguing that music wasn't only a receptacle for the true and untamed spirit of the folk, but also the foundation that kept its political edifices erect. In primordial times, Attali argued provocatively, a society dedicated to human sacrifice sought a way to cleanse itself of the violence it understood was likely, if left uncontrolled, to tear it asunder. It settled on music, which it understood as a stand-in for ritual murder. Music, Attali continued, terrified and enchanted our ancestors; rather than communicate directly and immediately, the way words did, music was seen as an interruption, a senseless squeal that released the same sort of emotions previously reserved for the altar and the knife. And with that, civilization was born, music helping it sublimate its fundamental brutalities. It's a wild notion, but Attali found echoes of it in the story of Ulysses and his sirens, as well as in the works of the Han Dynasty historian Sima Qian, who wrote that "the sacrifices and music, the rites and the laws have a single aim; it is through them that the hearts of the people are united, and it is from them that the method of good government arises."[11]

But music, Attali argued, didn't merely ossify or retreat into the realm of ancient practices, no longer understood. It continued to shape society. The troubadours who roamed Renaissance Europe and understood themselves to be a professional class of musicians, he wrote, provided one of the earliest indications that their society was moving away from a feudal order, rooted in land and blood and tradition, and toward a form of capitalism, which called for well-trained artisans. Finally, when music shifted once again, from the troubadours to the recording artists, from the live performance to the LP, it signaled yet another turn, into a new and predatory order of mechanized production. It was time for a fourth thrust, Attali wrote, never expanding too much on what that new prophetic age might look like or what it might say about society and its direction.

The question, however, was best left not to theoreticians but to musicians themselves. Dylan said it best when he claimed that "the times" were "a-changin'." And, to the extent that he explicitly considered his mission, his lyrics suggest that he understood it to be, along the lines of Attali's ideas, part of an endeavor designed to propel society to higher planes. Cohen wanted to do the same. The less confidence he had in words, the more enthusiastic he was about music. Seeing Dylan search for the hidden face of God with his guitar was all the reassurance he needed to take the same step.

It wasn't an easy one. Committed to his new career choice, Cohen left Hydra and moved to New York City. He rented an apartment downtown for Marianne and Axel, but he himself lived in a series of hotels, the last and best known of which was the Chelsea. Never feeling at home at home, he took comfort in hotel life. "You always have the feeling in a hotel room that you're on the lam, and it's one of the safe moments in the escape," he told a documentary crew following him. "It's a breathing spot. The hotel room is the oasis of the downtown, it's a kind of a refuge, a sanctuary, a sanctuary of a temporary kind and therefore all the more delicious. But whenever I come into a hotel room, there's a moment, after the door is shut, and the lights you haven't turned on illumine a very comfortable, anonymous, subtly hostile environment, and you know that you found a little place in the grass, and the hounds are going to go by for three more hours. You're going to have a drink, light a cigarette, and take a long time shaving."[12]

There was little such tranquillity at the Chelsea. Run by David Bard and his son Stanley, Hungarian Jews with a talent for tolerance—and blessed with thick walls—it was the perfect haven for the short moment that became New York's bohemia. Arthur Miller, who lived there for a spell a few years before Cohen arrived, recalled what it was like to live amid the chaos: "It was thrilling to know that Virgil Thomson was writing his nasty music reviews on the top floor, and that those canvases hanging over the lobby were by Larry Rivers, no doubt as rent, and that the hollow-cheeked girl on the elevator was Viva and the hollow-eyed man with her was Warhol and that scent you caught was marijuana."[13]

It was not an auspicious scene for a young poet with a guitar hesitantly taking his first steps as a musician. The world Leonard Cohen had most likely imagined he would inhabit, echoes of which were audible on Dylan's early records, was fading, and a new one, white hot, was emerging. There are many ways to explain the change in popular music between 1965, the year Cohen discovered Dylan, and 1966, the year Cohen presented himself in New York to begin his new incarnation as singer, but, as is so often the case when contemplating the history of rock and roll, none is more effective than simply listening to the Beatles. In December 1965 the band, already understood to be rock incarnate, released *Rubber Soul*. The album has many hits, and each is easy to place within a distinct tradition. The steely guitar lick that launches "Drive My Car" is as showy and exuberant and good-natured as anything by Chuck Berry, whose "Roll Over, Beethoven" the Beatles had covered two years before. "You Won't See Me," for all its cantankerous breakup lyrics, "was very Motown-flavored," Paul McCartney said of the song.[14] Listen to the song's bass line, and you can imagine you're listening to the Four Tops or the Temptations. Even the intensely intimate and sweetly melancholic "In My Life" was more a traditional composition than a sui generis autobiography. As the band's biographer Bob Spitz notes, the song began its life as a nostalgic rough draft composed by John Lennon and was then handed over to McCartney, who wrote the melody "based on a Smokey Robinson motif, 'with the minors and little harmonies' lifted from Miracles records."[15] All of this, of course, is not to say that the Beatles are somehow less deserving of their eternal glory; it's only to note that in 1965 they were a monumental band that worked squarely within a musical tradition it knew well and respected. Nine months later, that changed.

Revolver, the Beatles' next UK release, came out in August 1966. From the very first track, "Taxman," the album declared war on everything that had come before. The song's lyrics, complaining about the steep taxes the band had to pay on its considerable earnings, are sharp and caustic, a far cry from the love-me-dos of 1962. And the guitars are grating, the result of the recording tape having been fed into the recorder and played backward, a new effect the Beatles discovered during the making of *Revolver* and used giddily and often. "Eleanor Rigby"—a symphonic production for four violins, two violas, and two cellos—was recorded with microphones placed very close to the instruments, giving the song a raw sound. And the album's last song, "Tomorrow Never Knows," is a single C-chord played by George Harrison on a tamboura with a repetitively beating drum and Lennon's voice routed from the recording console into the studio's speaker to accommodate the singer's request that he sound "like the Dalai Lama and thousands of Tibetan monks chanting on a mountain top."[16] In other words, *Revolver* sounded like nothing else.

And it was hardly alone. 1966 was the year of transforming sound. In May, Dylan was booed as a Judas for taking the stage at Manchester's Free Trade Hall backed up by the Hawks, electric guitars and all. In July he crashed his Triumph motorcycle near his home in Woodstock and stopped performing for nearly a decade. The Rolling Stones introduced the sitar on "Paint It, Black," while the 13th Floor Elevators played the electric jug on their influential first album.

New instruments and new recording techniques were all de rigueur, but new ideas were more important: Staying home as his brothers toured Japan, Brian Wilson, hopped up on acid and Eastern thought, wrote most of *Pet Sounds*, the Beach Boys' masterpiece. With lyrics musing about the fragility of the ego backed up by bass harmonicas and banjos, the album was as much a philosophical triumph as a musical achievement. Together with *Revolver* it heralded the psychedelic era, declaring that rock was less interested in harmonies and aesthetics than it was in consciousness and its limits, in trance and transcendence.

There was nothing inherently strange about rock and roll's heady turn. Art forms, after all, mature like every other living thing, spending their early years learning boundaries before developing a sense of self that ripens with time. But rock seemed to have come of age overnight. One day Lennon was the cheeky boy with the bowl cut and the pretty love songs; the next he was telling Maureen Cleave of the London *Evening Standard* that his band and the whole genre he represented were destined to replace other, ancient, more established forms of faith. "Christianity will go," he said. "It will vanish and sink. I needn't argue about that. I'm right and will be proved right. We're more popular than Jesus now."[17] The statement sparked controversy, and Lennon was forced to apologize, but most of his detractors failed to realize just how sincere the Beatle had been. He wasn't a bored rock star flippantly bragging about his fame; he was stating the unofficial credo of the annus mirabilis of 1966, namely that rock was not entertainment but something closer to religion, a path to salvation paved by bass, guitar, and drums.

It was hardly an original idea. It informed much of religious life prior to the dawn of Christianity, with cults whose celebrations relied heavily on music as a conduit of ecstasy. The Eleusinian Mysteries ceremonies, held annually for millennia to celebrate Demeter, the goddess of the harvest, included the ingesting of hallucinogenic substances, trancelike dancing, loud music, and lewd behavior, the very elements that were now said to be corrupting the souls of the young. Music's power did not diminish with the rise of the church: Augustine, despite heeding Plato's warning about the temptations of poetry, performance, and music, nonetheless found them to be a great spiritual engine. In his *Confessions* he described a moment of elation that occurred whenever he attended church and heard a moving hymn. "The music surged in my ears," he wrote, "truth seeped into my heart, and feelings of devotion overflowed."[18] The same sentiment is expressed in Romans, which informs us that "faith cometh by hearing, and hearing by the word of God."[19] The most seminal Jewish prayer is the Shema ("hear"), which begins "Hear, O Israel, the Lord our God is one Lord."[20] Of all the senses at our disposal, it is hearing—rather than vision or touch or smell—that connects us to the divine.

Theology and musicology both have much to say about this fact, but they agree on two foundational insights. First, music is paramount because, like human existence, it is experienced first and foremost through the passage of time. "Because we live through time," wrote the American theologian Don E. Saliers, "music is perhaps our most natural medium for coming to terms with time, and attending to the transcendent elements in making sense of our temporality. Our lives, like music, have pitch, tempo, tone, release, dissonance, harmonic convergence, as we move through times of grief, delight, hope, anger, and joy. In short, music has this deep affinity to our spiritual temperament and desire. Our lives, like music, can be understood in remembering the passage through time. The order of sound is comprehended as we remember and re-configure the previously heard in light of the yet-to-be-heard. So, too, the deeper desires and yearnings of the human soul are not understood until a larger pattern emerges."[21] And that larger pattern, in faith and music alike, revolves around tension and resolution. "The word of promise," the German theologian Jürgen Moltmann observed, "always creates an interval of tension between the uttering and the redeeming of the promise. In so doing it provides man with a peculiar area of freedom to obey or disobey, to be hopeful or resigned."[22] That peculiar area of promise is the one in which the faithful live—the Christian awaiting the return of Christ, the Jew yearning, in the words of the Passover Haggadah, for next year in Jerusalem. But it is also the area in which music is endowed with meaning. Think of the final minute of the Beatles' "A Day in the Life." The orchestral crescendos create an unbearable tension; by the time the forty-second-long E-major final chord crashes against our eardrums, we welcome it as redemption.

And by 1966 redemption—of mind, of soul, of body—was what rock and roll was after. Which might have fitted nicely with the designs of a poet interested in prophecy, but the scene wasn't kind to Leonard Cohen. He visited agent after agent and was denied. He was too old, his songs too sad. Finally, through a friend, he was referred to a fellow Canadian named Mary Martin, who worked for Bob Dylan's manager, Albert Grossman. Martin made the necessary introductions, and by November of that year, two of Cohen's first compositions were recorded by Judy Collins on her breakthrough album, *In My Life*. One was called "Dress Rehearsal Rag"; the other was "Suzanne," an early poem set to music. The album went gold almost immediately, and Cohen could now claim himself a songwriter—the others whose work Collins had covered on *In My Life* included Dylan, the Beatles, and Randy Newman. Still, he found New York inhospitable.

"I was looking for the revolutionary expression of the brotherhood of man," he told *Mojo* magazine decades later. "I was going to be able to feel tangibly this new world. I've always been up for those things. Then I heard that everything was happening in the East Village, so I went there. It seemed a terribly messy, filthy place but I was game. I went into one coffee shop after another and felt frozen out, just like in Montreal."[23] In one place, frustrated and lonely, he scribbled the words "KILL COOL" on a place mat; no one paid him any mind.[24]

And why would they? Cohen didn't look or act like anyone primed to make an impression in New York in 1966. At La Dom, a club on Eighth Street that was lined with silver tinfoil and owned by the silver-haired Warhol, Cohen met Nico, who seemed to him like "the apotheosis of the Nazi earth mother,"[25] and a jittery, skinny boy who played in a band Warhol was managing and who had some ideas of his own about the future of rock and roll. When they first met, Lou Reed surprised Cohen by expressing his admiration for *Flowers for Hitler*. But Reed's ideas weren't Leonard Cohen's: Reed, like everybody else who helped make 1966 the year of rock rapture, wanted to burn everything that had come before. He was given the chance to express his view in a four-page essay titled "The View from the Bandstand," printed on pink paper and enclosed in the third volume of the multimedia magazine *Aspen*. Having already written many of the songs that, a few months later, would appear on *The Velvet Underground and Nico* and make him rock's grittiest poet, Reed took to his manifesto with all the roughness characteristic of his work at the time but none of the sublime tenderness that enabled him to come up with lines about a heroin user feeling just like Jesus's son. He was mainly interested in insults. Cole Porter, he wrote in *Aspen*, was nothing more than a purveyor of "cheap cocktail sentiment." Pat Boone made "bullshit music." Classical music was so simple, "anyone can write it." Robert Lowell was a bore undeserving of his laurels. And everywhere you looked in American culture, you saw nothing but death. "Writing was dead, movies were dead. Everybody sat like an unpeeled orange." There was beautiful music before, even some decent rock and roll, but it was fake, "manufactured so it could be taught. It was a myth perpetrated by pedants seeking tenure." But now rock was finally awakening, with the Beatles and the Beach Boys and the Who and the Velvet Underground bringing it all back home. "The music," Reed concluded, "is sex and drugs and happy."[26]

In other words, the music was cool. But Cohen wasn't. The songs he was working on in his hotel room, rehearsing in front of a large mirror, had nothing in common with the zeitgeist. Reed was reading Oswald Spengler and reveling in the thought of Western civilization's inevitable decline; Brian Wilson was reading Arthur Koestler and thinking hard about metaphysics; and Cohen was still the boy who'd listened to Isaiah and written lines about it being hard to hold the hand of anyone who's reaching to the sky just to surrender, and about us forgetting to pray for the angels and the angels forgetting to pray for us. There was nothing of the Age of Aquarius in Cohen's lyrics, and even less of it in his tunes, strange and hypnotic melodies that droned on softly. He traveled back and forth between New York and Canada, spending months on each of his songs, getting into his lifelong habit of writing dozens of verses for each one and then slowly trimming them down to their bare essence. He partook in the drug culture, and noted that it failed to do for him what it had done for John Lennon or Brian Wilson or Lou Reed. Frustrated, he wrote barbed bits of poetry. "I am so impatient," read one, written in March 1967, "I cannot / even read slowly. I never really loved to learn. / I want to live alone / in fellowship with men. / I'm telling you this because / secret agreements bring / misfortune."[27]

Eventually Mary Martin called and asked him out to lunch. They'd be dining, she said, with John Hammond, the man who had discovered Billie Holiday and Aretha Franklin and, most important, just six years earlier, Dylan. Martin, Hammond later recalled, had called him up and said, "John, there's this poet from Canada, who I think you'd be interested in. He plays pretty good guitar, and he's a wonderful songwriter, but he doesn't read music, and he's sort of very strange. I don't think Columbia would be at all interested in him, but you might be."[28] His curiosity piqued, Hammond went to see Cohen at the Chelsea; he took him to a nearby restaurant, ordered a generous lunch, and made sure to talk about everything but music. Then he looked at Leonard and said, "Let's go back to the hotel, and maybe you'll play me some songs." Back in his room, stealing glances at his mirror as he strummed to help overcome his anxiety, Cohen played "Suzanne," "The Stranger Song," "Master Song," and "Hey, That's No Way to Say Goodbye."

Hammond was immediately convinced. "I thought he was enchanting," he recalled. "That's the only word you can use. He was not like anything I've ever heard before. I just feel that I always want a true original, if I can find one, because there are not many in the world. And the young man set his own rules, and he was a really first-class poet, which is most important."[29] When Cohen put down his guitar, Hammond simply said, "You got it," leaving Cohen to wonder whether it referred to God-given talent or the more earthly reward of a recording contract with Columbia. Hammond had probably meant both, and in August 1967 Cohen entered the studio to record his debut album.

There was no trace in him of the ebullient young man who'd declared to his fellow Canadian poets that he was off to become the next Dylan. As his fantasy slouched closer to fruition, doubts began to emerge. A few months earlier, on April 30, Judy Collins had invited him to join her onstage at a concert to protest the Vietnam War, held in Town Hall. "Suzanne" was her hit, but backstage Collins told Cohen he should step into the spotlight and sing his song.

"I can't do it, Judy," he replied. "I would die from embarrassment."

Collins pleaded, assuring Cohen he was "a great writer and a fine singer" and that people wanted to hear him. Reluctantly, he agreed, and Collins went onstage to introduce her friend. Cohen followed. "He walked onto the stage hesitantly," Collins remembered, "his guitar slung across his hips, and from the wings I could see his legs shaking inside his trousers." Cohen started playing, but by the time he got to the bit about the tea and the oranges that come all the way from China he suddenly stopped. "I can't go on," he said, and rushed offstage.

Surprised, the audience remained silent for a few moments, and then responded by clapping loudly and shouting at Cohen that they loved him and that he was great, urging him to come back. Standing backstage, his head resting on Judy Collins's shoulder, Cohen muttered that he couldn't do it, he couldn't go back.

"He looked about ten years old," Collins recalled. "His mouth drew down at the sides, he started to untangle himself from his guitar strap. I stopped him, touching him on the shoulder. 'But you will,' I said. He shook himself and drew his body up and put his shoulders back, smiled again, and walked back onto the stage. He finished 'Suzanne,' and the audience went wild."[30]

It was a strange turn for someone like Cohen, accustomed to hamming it up onstage, reading his verse out loud, and telling stories. Clutching his poetry collections, charming college students, Cohen was confident. With his guitar, alone, he was terrified. Perhaps he truly felt that his songs were, as he often referred to them, a diary set to guitar music, something much too intimate to share. Perhaps performing onstage called on faculties—a pleasant voice, physical prowess—that were not among Cohen's greatest gifts. Whatever the reason, Cohen's emergence as a singer was dramatically different from his ascendance as a poet. In his youth he had adopted Layton's dictum that all a young poet needed to make it was ignorance and an exaggerated sense of self. But as a man in his thirties, he was much too self-aware not to realize that he was playing a game whose rules were deeply foreign.

Four months after the Town Hall concert, entering Columbia's studios to record his album, the same anxiety struck again. John Hammond did his best to keep the nervous young artist at ease. The studio he had chosen, Studio E, was small and cozy, and Hammond had it lit by candles and made sure the air was thick with incense. From his spot behind the console, Hammond shouted merrily into the studio's speaker, "Watch out, Dylan!," and then unfolded his newspaper and read it as Cohen played. It was a ploy to keep the budding musician at ease; it didn't succeed. Cohen asked that a full-length mirror be brought to the studio, so he could sing to it as he'd sung to his mirror at the Chelsea, a dilettante amusing himself. A mirror soon materialized. It did little to calm Cohen down.

The problem was the others in the room. Cohen, his experience playing with others limited to doing bar mitzvahs with the Buckskin Boys, had no idea how to play music with professionals. "When I first went into the studio," he later recalled, "John Hammond arranged for me to play with four or five dynamite New York studio musicians. Those takes were lively, but I kept listening to what the musicians were doing. It was the first time I had ever played with a really accomplished band, and I was somewhat intimidated by this. I didn't really know how to sing with a band. I really didn't know how to sing with really good, professional musicians that were really cooking. And I would tend to listen to the musicians, rather than concentrate on what I was doing, because they were doing it so much more proficiently than I was."[31] Someone, then, had to serve as a liaison between Cohen and the band, and Hammond hired Willie Ruff, an Alabama-born bass and French horn player who taught music at Yale. A linguist by training, Ruff appreciated Cohen's lyrics, and didn't much mind that he couldn't read music. He kept the time, and kept Cohen focused on delivering his song.

And then Hammond left. His other commitments to younger, more commercially appealing artists routinely drew him away from the odd, older musician in Studio E, and Cohen, tired of waiting, demanded a full-time producer. The task was eventually assigned to John Simon, a talented musician who had a number two hit on the Billboard chart in 1966 with "Red Rubber Ball," a song the young Paul Simon had written for the band the Cyrkle. The first thing John Simon noticed was the way Cohen played guitar. "He wasn't a guitar player like most of the artists I was working with," he later recalled. "Most of the artists grew up listening to pop music, so they knew how to play rock 'n' roll or something like that. Leonard, apparently, learned how to play classical guitar,"[32] which meant that rather than simply strum, as they did in pop, or fingerpick, as they did in folk, he played something closer to the Spanish *rasgueado*, the rapid and precise style of flamenco that was based on fast little jagged phrases. "Journalists were very cruel to me," Cohen commented when asked about the general perception that he wasn't much of a musician. "They said I only knew three chords when I knew five."[33]

But his distinct style wasn't what soon put him on a collision course with Simon. An astute and experienced producer, Simon believed that Cohen's songs needed sweetening. They were spare, almost harsh, and needed "strings and assorted pillows of sound for Cohen's voice to rest on."[34] To save "Suzanne" from droning, Simon suggested drums; Cohen objected. Simon tried for a different sort of syncopation, and brought in a piano player. Cohen insisted that the piano be removed. The song, he said, "should be linear, should be smooth."[35] With "So Long, Marianne" Simon thought the song would benefit from the treatment, popular at the time, of stopping it for a moment and then launching back into the chorus. Cohen hated the effect and removed it in the final mix. "It doesn't work," he said. "You can't just stop the song and start it again. What for? Just to make it hip?"[36] Someone—it's unclear who—suggested that female voices be used in lieu of instruments, which only underscored the flatness of Cohen's own vocals. Finally Simon gave up. "Look, Leonard," he said, "this is as far as I'm going to work on the record. I'm going on Christmas vacation. You finish it."[37]

Removing Simon's sweetening from the four-track master tape "was like trying to take the sugar back out of the coffee."[38] The result was haunting. Listening to the album, you can hear strings, cymbals, a whole menagerie of instruments, all playing softly, faintly, in the background, lacerated by Cohen's guitar.

The disjointed production, however, was plagued by much more than artistic differences or the jitters of a first-time singer. At its heart was a metaphysical problem: the problem of taking a spiritual vision and translating it into words and chords so that others listening would instantly understand its meaning.

The difficulty started with the lyrics. Ever since he had started writing songs, Cohen's method involved coming up with an avalanche of verses, then removing the unsalvageable ones and smoothing the ones he decided to keep. It took months, even years, and it was more than a mere editing job: As he pruned his verses, Cohen transformed them from personal confessions to universal invocations.

There's no clearer example of this, perhaps, than "Chelsea Hotel No. 2," one of his more autobiographical works, which Cohen has revealed—having since regretted his indiscretion—was about his dalliance with Janis Joplin. Before there was a "No. 2," however, there was a "No. 1," written sometime in the spring of 1972. It begins as we now know it, with Joplin talking brave and sweet and giving Cohen head on the unmade bed. Then there's a slow refrain, about Joplin making her "sweet little sounds." Then comes the confession: "I remember you well / In the Chelsea Hotel / In the winter of '67 / My friends of that year / They were all getting queer / And me, I was just getting even." And on it goes, with Cohen singing about going down to Tennessee and spending time with local legend Willie York and feeding peafowl and watching the stream. There's one more refrain, and Cohen admits that he's tired and signs off with "Guess I got nothing more to say to you, baby."[39]

By the time Cohen entered the studio to record the song for his fourth album, *New Skin for the Old Ceremony*, in the winter of 1974, Willie York and the peafowl and all those treacherous friends and the vindictive Leonard were all gone. Cohen kept the same premise—he and Joplin entwined on a bed at the Chelsea—but managed to distill the song to its purest essence. "And clenching your fist for the ones like us / Who are oppressed by the figures of beauty," go the final lyrics, "You fixed yourself, you said, 'Well never mind / We are ugly, but we have the music.'" What began as a biographical sketch turned into a mantra that the arty, dreamy kids infatuated with Cohen—never the libidinous hordes who bobbed to the Beatles or swayed to the Stones—could recite when times got dark: "We are ugly, but we have the music." Perhaps no line of Cohen's better captures the essence of his vision. He is telling his listeners what prophetically inclined rabbis had been telling theirs for thousands of years, namely that the world is a place of suffering, that no celestial cataclysm could ever change that, but that there are things here on this earth—art, love, friendship, kindness, music, sex—that have the power to redeem us.

When John Simon first met Leonard Cohen, the exact nature of the singer's work was lost on the young producer. Dylan, he said, was "the flavor of the year at that time, introspective songs that weren't necessarily about jilted lovers and those things." At first glance Cohen's words seemed to him squarely Dylan-esque, lyrics that "were so clouded and obfuscated you really didn't know what the hidden meaning is. I wasn't inclined to dig too deeply."[40] The comparison between Cohen and Dylan is instructive, and it reveals how radically different they are in their approach to text. Dylan, crudely speaking, has three modes of delivery. He is most famous for being gnomic—"met a young girl, she gave me a rainbow"[41]—and equally as famous for refusing to parse the meaning of his verse. Then there's Dylan the balladeer: "When they were singing years ago," Dylan told an interviewer in 1969, "it would be as entertainment . . . a fellow could sit down and sing a song for a half hour, and everybody could listen, and you could form opinions. You'd be waiting to see how it ended, what happened to this person or that person. It would be like going to a movie. But now we have movies, so why does someone want to sit around for a half hour listening to a ballad? Unless the story was of such a nature that you couldn't find it in a movie. And after you heard it, it would have to be good enough so that you could sing it again tomorrow night, and people would be listening to hear the story again. It's because they want to hear the story, not because they want to check out the singer's pants. Because they would have conscious knowledge of how the story felt and they would be a part of that feeling . . . like they would want to feel it again, so to speak."[42] That's how "The Lonesome Death of Hattie Carroll" or "The Ballad of Hollis Brown" or "Hurricane" work—they're stories engineered to produce immediate and fierce emotion. Anyone who hears about Hattie Carroll cleaning the table she'll never get to eat off of can't help but feel anything but rage. Finally there's Dylan the moralizer, a position that made the young singer popular and that the older singer abandoned, to the chagrin of many of his fans. In songs like "With God on Our Side" and "Masters of War," Dylan's message is as powerful as it is unambiguous.

Whatever mode Dylan was writing in, however, he was still being Dylan, which meant being a vessel to thoughts and ideas that swirled around him. He didn't like reading, he told an interviewer in the late 1960s; "I tried to read," he said, "but I usually would lay the book down. I never have been a fast reader. My thoughts weren't about reading, no . . . they were just about that feeling that was in the air."[43] Dylan was sharp and fast enough to trap these thoughts on the page. Talking about writing "Like a Rolling Stone," for example, he said, "I found myself writing this song, this story, this long piece of vomit, twenty pages long, and out of it I took 'Like a Rolling Stone' and made it a single. And I'd never written anything like that before and it suddenly came to me that this is what I should do."[44] "Vomit" is a vulgar but effective metaphor; Dylan's words just streamed out. In the late 1980s, he met Leonard Cohen backstage after Cohen performed in Paris, and praised "Hallelujah," asking Cohen how long it had taken to write. It had taken Cohen years, but not wishing to come off as the tortured and exacting artist, he lied and told Dylan it had taken a year or two. Then it was Cohen's turn to praise one of his favorite Dylan songs, "I and I," and ask how long it had taken to write. Dylan replied it had taken fifteen minutes.[45]

The comparison with Dylan is even more instructive when we think about Leonard Cohen's sound. Dylan was as freewheeling with his music as he was with his words.

He had Muddy Waters and Odetta and Woody Guthrie and a whole gallery of musicians he considered authentically American to draw on, which gave him a natural sound no matter how playful or poetic he was being. He has made that point in song—as much, that is, as one can refer to what an artist, especially Bob Dylan, does as argumentation—when he crooned, in his 2009 album *Together Through Life*, that he had "the blood of the land" in his voice.[46] "For more than half a century," Sean Wilentz poignantly writes about him, "Bob Dylan had been absorbing, transmuting, and renewing and improving American art forms long thought to be trapped in formal conventions. He not only 'put folk into bed with rock,' as Al Santos still announces before each concert; he took traditional folk music, the blues, rock and roll, country and western, black gospel, Tin Pan Alley, Tex-Mex borderlands music, Irish outlaw ballads, and more and bent them to his own poetic muse."[47]

Cohen, too, grew up absorbing a wide array of musical styles, listening to Ray Charles and Hank Williams and his mother's Russian lullabies and Jacques Brel, but he was no Dylan. When he entered the studio he had no interest in playing with forms. Instead he sought to fashion the form that would best serve his words. And that form was always austere.

In the studio, recording *Songs of Leonard Cohen*, John Simon found the songs as Cohen played them depressing. He was in awe of Cohen—having invited the singer to spend the weekend at his parents' house in Connecticut, Simon woke up in the morning to discover that Cohen had stayed up all night browsing the books in the home's vast library—and believed philosophically that a producer must always defer to the artist.

But he still wanted "to try and dress him up a little bit, to put a little icing on the cake."[48] Icing, he thought, was all the cake needed: the songs were sad, but they were also beautiful, and their beauty had to be accentuated. Simon brought in the singer Nancy Priddy to sing background vocals. "They were poignant songs," he recalled, "but to have harmony makes it more universal, people identify with that."[49]

But that wasn't enough for Simon. He listened to the songs and tried to glean their meaning. Operating on the assumption that Cohen, like Dylan, had incoherent visions that needed much interpreting, he let his imagination run wild. "Sisters of Mercy," for example, evoked "the sense of nuns, the sense of the Red Cross, some healing operation that was pulling in, some mobile healing operation that was pulling into town."[50] To capture this mental image of kindly nurses riding in an ethereal ambulance, Simon wheeled a hurdy-gurdy into the studio; its sound, he hoped, would convey a sense of motion, of carnival, of streets.

Cohen wanted it all taken out, and, as it couldn't be altogether removed, relegated it to the background. The hurdy-gurdy is still faintly audible, but Cohen's cut had no room for imaginative interpretations. The song didn't need them. The song was not, as Dylan once said of his compositions, "a commercial item" akin to "boats and brooms,"[51] something that people bought and sold and therefore something that needed to be produced and marketed to listeners. The song was an invocation of the *duende*, and as such needed nothing but those repeated eighth-note triplets on the guitar and Cohen's voice slowly reciting the words: "You who must leave everything that you cannot control / It begins with your family, but soon it comes round to your soul / Well, I've been where you're hanging, I think I can see how you're pinned / When you're not feeling holy, your loneliness says that you've sinned." It's the kind of message—not immediately uplifting, not immediately understood—that needs the lightest musical accompaniment. Whatever else Cohen was uncertain of in Studio E, of that he was sure.

Others were less convinced. When the album came out, the *New York Times* titled its review "Alienated Young Man Creates Some Sad Music." Cohen, wrote the esteemed critic Donal Henahan, "sounds like a sad man cashing in on self-pity and adolescent loneliness," selling "Weltschmerz and soft rock" that placed him "somewhere between Schopenhauer and Bob Dylan" on the alienation scale. But whereas Dylan "is alienated from society and mad about it, Mr. Cohen is alienated and merely sad about it," a troubadour "smooth of voice and bland of meaning."[52] Surprisingly, Cohen's actual voice appealed to another harsh critic, *Rolling Stone*'s Arthur Schmidt: "It is a strange voice," Schmidt wrote, "he hits every note, but between each note he recedes to an atonal place—his songs are thus given a sorely needed additional rhythm."[53] Still, Schmidt captured the critical consensus when he judged the album a very mixed bag. "I don't think I could ever tolerate all of it," he wrote. "There are three brilliant songs, one good one, three qualified bummers, and three are the flaming shits."[54] The reader is invited to guess which is which.

The reviews seem to have left Cohen in a somber state of mind. When a *New York Times* reporter came over for a profile piece, Cohen stood by his window at the Chelsea and pretended to contemplate jumping.[55] He brought up suicide again when

Richard Goldstein showed up to interview him for the *Village Voice*. "Today he faces me across a hotel room with the sun shining second hand in the windows down the block," Goldstein wrote of Cohen. "The drapes are as florid as his verse."[56] Cohen himself must have sensed his interrogator's disdain, as he spent most of the conversation recounting failures real and imagined, before offering a morbid coda. "Around 30 or 35 is the traditional age for the suicide of the poet," he said. "That's the age when you finally understand that the universe does not succumb to your command."[57]

The universe abided, leaving Cohen, at thirty-four, with a small coterie of devoted fans and modest commercial success but no cataclysmic sense of transformation. He was a singer now, but few people listened. Worse, it was the Age of Aquarius, and in art and politics alike, the prophetic undertaking seemed to be somewhat of a national pastime. Among the lithe and the loud who sought a musical path to transcendence, what chance did an older and timorous and slight stranger really have?

CHAPTER SIX

Waiting for the Sun

I n 1969 Leonard Cohen met Bob Dylan for the first time. Curious about the young Canadian singer, Dylan summoned Cohen to the Kettle of Fish, the MacDougal Street joint where he spent many evenings drinking. No record survives, but it is reasonable to assume that pleasantries were uttered and mutual admirations exchanged. Six years later things were very different.

By 1975 Dylan was a man once again transformed. He was separating from his wife, Sara, was warring with both his manager and his record label, and was feeling as if he was going "down, down, down . . . I was convinced I wasn't going to do anything else."[1] It was like a sudden attack of amnesia, he said; "I couldn't learn what I had been able to do naturally—like *Highway 61 Revisited*. I mean, you can't sit down and write that consciously because it has to do with the break-up of time."[2] He wanted to do something to shake off the doldrums; the only thing he could think of was a circus.

It hit the road in late October, calling itself the Rolling Thunder Revue. Dylan wore whiteface makeup, and sometimes a mask. Joan Baez was invited to sing along—appearing onstage with Dylan for the first time in years—as was Ramblin' Jack Elliott, Woody Guthrie's disciple and musical scion. Mick Ronson, David Bowie's ace guitarist, was there, too, as was Scarlet Rivera, an unknown violinist Dylan had discovered when he saw her walking down the street in Manhattan's Lower East Side. Sam Shepard was appointed the tour's official documentarian, Allen Ginsberg its lyrical rabbi. The old folkies and the new glam rockers, the celebrated and the unknown—this was Dylan's idea of a big tent. He made sure the music was just as carnivalesque: Whereas with the Band he had delivered straight-up rock and roll, the Revue crew inspired mischief, taking "It Ain't Me, Babe" a step away from reggae or "A Hard Rain's A-Gonna Fall" into a cheery, fast-paced, hard-edged blues riff.

The Revue had many charms, but it was, as much as anything else, a sweet surrender. Dylan remained—remains—as blessed as ever, consistently producing superb albums, but by the time he mounted his musical circus, it was hard not to feel as if the man taking the stage was more committed to interpretation than to invention. Like those Western towns that popped up with the gold rush and were abandoned when the shiny mineral failed to materialize or was fully harvested, Dylan's music, having once promised great spiritual riches to those brave enough to mine it, was now a historical curiosity, a tourist attraction, a good place to visit for a while before driving back home and forgetting all about it the following day.

As the first leg of the Revue neared its end, in December 1975, Dylan et al. rolled into Montreal, and the ringmaster ordered Larry "Ratso" Sloman, a journalist who tagged along for the ride, to call Cohen and ask him to join the festivities. Sloman did, but Cohen sounded weary. "Is it going to be crowded?" he asked.

"You won't have to deal with the crowds," Sloman assured him. "We'll zip in the stage door, Leonard."

Listening to the conversation, Dylan grew restless. He grabbed the receiver from Sloman and asked Cohen how he was doing. Cohen replied that he couldn't complain.

"Can't complain, huh," Dylan said. "Well I could but I won't. You wanna come to the show?" Cohen said he did. Dylan asked if he would join the band onstage and play a few songs. Cohen said something elusive. Dylan didn't press. Later that evening Sloman was sent to pick Cohen up from his apartment; he was riding in a cab with Sara, Dylan's wife, and asked the driver to wait a moment while he ran up to get Cohen. Entering Cohen's apartment, however, he found the singer surrounded by friends, playing the harmonica, stomping his feet, and bellowing a French chanson. Sloman urged Cohen to hurry. Cohen responded by sipping wine. Then more song, more banter. When Cohen finally made his way into the car, Sara asked him if he was going to sing. "No," he responded. "Are you?"

By the time the car pulled into the Montreal Forum, Sloman had pleaded with Cohen three more times, and Cohen cheerfully responded by bursting into another French ditty. Backstage, Joni Mitchell, having just finished her set, ran up to Cohen and hugged him, followed shortly by Dylan himself. With the master of ceremonies now present, Sloman tried one more time.

"Hey, Leonard, you gonna sing," he said, less a question than a plea.

"I'm going to sit out there and watch," Cohen said.

"Why not sing?" asked Mitchell.

"No, no, it's too obvious," Cohen replied, and made his way to a line of folding chairs nearby, where he sat down just in time to see Dylan take the stage.[3]

Cohen's refusal to humor the man who had influenced him so greatly is baffling. It is possible, of course, that Cohen, always reluctant to perform, particularly when unaccompanied by his band, felt that the burden of entertaining the tens of thousands of fans who crowded the Forum was just too much. It is also possible that he and Dylan had let their relationship grow cold. They had experienced some awkwardness five years earlier, after Dylan's producer, Bob Johnston, decamped to work with Cohen instead. But Cohen's explanation suggests another, more profound possibility: Taking the stage *would* have been too obvious, an admission, perhaps, that he, too, subscribed to Dylan's approach, thought of his own songs as objects no different than brooms and boats, and was ready to repackage them for a rapidly shifting market. That was not the case: By 1975 both Dylan and Cohen had noticed the strong tremors remapping the landscape of rock and roll, and both had understood that their shared sensibility—the one still rooted in folk music and still deeply dedicated to crafting fiery lyrics that attempted an account of human life, in all its frailty and glory—was no longer welcomed. New artists delivered bolder visions, peddling ecstasy whereas Dylan and Cohen promised only reflection. There were new prophets in town, and Dylan's response was to slather on a thick layer of white face paint, go on tour, and revel in obfuscation; if kids these days want their music loud and psychedelic, you can imagine him reasoning, I'll show them by forcing all my tender songs to wear grotesque masks.

But Cohen could not follow suit. In the three albums he'd recorded since his debut, he went the opposite route. His second album, *Songs from a Room*, recorded in Nashville and released in 1969, was even starker than *Songs of Leonard Cohen* had been. Bob Johnston, the album's producer, believed that the best approach to cultivating sound was to intervene as little as possible. When the first recording session ended, Cohen, still concerned that he was not doing his compositions justice, came into the control room and asked Johnston what he wanted to do. Johnston said that he wanted to go get hamburgers and beer. When they came back, Cohen asked the same question, and Johnston said that the only thing he expected the singer to do was sing. Cohen did, and when he was done, he asked, uncertainly, "Is that what I'm supposed to sound like?"

"Yeah," Johnston said.[4] And he meant it. Songs like "Bird on the Wire" needed no adornment. In the liner notes to the album's 2007 rerelease, the song is described as being "simultaneously a prayer and an anthem." It is, but not in the traditional sense. Anthems are heroic and collective, designed to inspire individual hearts to swell with patriotic pride by evoking shared history or extolling common symbols. Prayers, on the other hand, are both intensely personal—they are, after all, designed as a direct, if not reciprocal, conversation between the believer and his God—and entirely generic. The Amidah, for example, the central prayer of Jewish liturgy, contains nineteen blessings, all of which address the welfare of the entire community. Observant Jews pray for God to be forgiving, petition him to hasten the coming of the messiah, and plead with him to bestow peace and kindness on all of his chosen people. The private vagaries of individual souls go unnoticed and unaddressed.

Not in Cohen's songs. In "Bird on the Wire," for example, there's a verse that describes, in plain language, two different encounters. "I saw a beggar leaning on his wooden crutch, / He said to me, 'You must not ask for so much.' / And a pretty woman leaning in her darkened door, / She cried to me, 'Hey, why not ask for more?'" They're delivered in the first person, making them feel intimate, as if Cohen was merely recalling something that had happened to him the other day. But, of course, there's much more to the song than that. It has a little bit of the prayer—"I swear by this song / And by all that I have done wrong / I will make it all up to thee"—and a little bit of the anthem—"I have tried in my way to be free"—but it is neither. It is first and foremost a confession of imperfections—Cohen's own—and then an exhortation never to lose sight of the beacons of beauty that break through even the thickest darkness. We may, like the song's narrator, inflict great suffering on ourselves and on others by being ungrateful and unkind, but, like him, too, we are never without our will. We are free to take the hand of the decrepit beggar and urge ourselves to desire less, or we can be seduced by the pretty woman's cry and allow ourselves to crave for more. Whichever we choose, it is nothing but our own personal path to freedom.

Rather than abandon his listeners, as Dylan had, to find their own way out of the thicket of his songs, Cohen wanted nothing standing between them and his words, removing all distractions, from ornate arrangements to excessively impenetrable verses. And whereas Dylan reveled in the playful and the surreal, Cohen was sincere and direct. "You who build these altars now, / to sacrifice these children,"—he sang in "The Story of Isaac," another of the album's notable songs—"you must not do it anymore." Dylan was never so heartfelt, even early in his career, when he was singing what some of his fans called protest songs.

Cohen's candor appealed—*Songs from a Room* did better than its predecessor, making his name known in Europe while selling modestly in the United States. But other ideas appealed far more. By 1969 Americans didn't want redemption negotiated somberly to the tune of a lonely guitar. They wanted it to come in bursts of sound, immediate, orgasmic. Put differently, they didn't want Leonard Cohen; they wanted Jim Morrison.

While comparing Cohen to Dylan was obvious and inevitable from the moment the former first became a singer, the affinities between Cohen and Morrison are less obvious but in many ways as illuminating. Like Cohen, Morrison was the son of a military officer, and like Cohen he found solace in poetry. One of his classmates at UCLA remembered[5] spending an evening in the library, where Morrison worked, listening to the future front man of the Doors—then a pudgy teen with a bad crew cut—talk endlessly about Oedipus. But whereas Cohen's transformation took a decade and fashioned him into a poet, an expatriate, and a novelist, Morrison's came overnight. Eve Babitz, a former girlfriend, recalled in a tribute that Morrison had spent one summer taking so many drugs that he emerged a changed man in the fall, trim and irresistible. She was writing on the occasion of Oliver Stone's 1991 biopic, *The Doors*, and criticized Stone's choice of lead actor. "According to everyone," she wrote, "Val Kilmer is supposed to have gotten Jim's looks exactly right, but what can Val Kilmer know of having been fat all of his life and suddenly one summer taking so much LSD and waking up a prince? Val Kilmer has always been a prince, so he can't have the glow; when you've never been a mud lark it's just not the same. And people these days, they don't know what it was to suddenly possess the power to fuck every single person you even idly fancied, they don't know the physical glamour of that—back when rock 'n roll was in flower and movies were hopelessly square."[6]

Morrison's music subscribed to the same logic of instant transformation. As a young man Morrison had read Arthur Rimbaud, and inherited from him the drug-addled, jagged yearning for bliss that could only be dreamed up from the depths of suffering. In his best-known work, *A Season in Hell*, Rimbaud cries, in a section dedicated to lamenting lost dreams and shattered hopes, "Let it come, let it come / The time when we fall in love." Every song by the Doors contains the same cries, embodied in Ray Manzarek's sepulchral organ. They sound like yelps from the crypt, emitted by some impatient creature eager to get out.

The Doors situated themselves in a strange place, not only musically but theologically as well. Music and religion both have an affinity for delay. "I consider that our present sufferings are not worth comparing with the glory that will be revealed in us," Christ says in Romans, "for the creation waits in eager expectation for the children of God to be revealed."[7] The Old and New Testaments alike are books of waiting; the humans who populate them speak of salvation and cataclysm, but more than anything they linger in anticipation for God to act.

The same goes for music: The best compositions set up complications and progress by slowly disentangling them. Beethoven's Fifth is probably the best example: It begins with a monumental blow, its ominous bars throwing us off balance. This, Beethoven told Anton Felix Schindler, his biographer, was the sound of destiny knocking at the door.[8] The rest of the symphony resolves the tension created by the first few notes. "What distinguishes superior creative musicians from the mediocre ones of all periods," the jazz scholar Leroy Ostransky wrote, "is the manner in which they create resolutions, and to create resolutions it is necessary to set up irresolutions."[9]

Without initial irresolutions, music—indeed, all art—loses much of its meaning. So does life: While we often tend to think of tension in negative terms, and are eager to eliminate it whenever it appears, it is a source of nuance and complexity that renders our lives rich. "Well-handled maintenance of tensions is ethically desired," the philosopher Kathleen Marie Higgins argues, and is "essential to living a balanced, happy life."[10] Without it we would either believe that we have supreme powers to bend the world to our will, or succumb to utter hopelessness and abandon all sense of agency. Music, Higgins writes, is instrumental in helping us reach a much-needed equilibrium, as it "presents tension, not as obstructions, but as themselves vehicles to the achievement of resolution."[11] In other words, to enjoy music, and to enjoy life, is to enjoy tension and see it not as a boulder blocking the path to a desirable goal but as the path itself.

Such insights were lost on Jim Morrison. For him the goal was always, to borrow one of his better-known lyrics, to "break on through to the other side." The Doors delivered nothing but resolutions. Nowhere, perhaps, was this more audible than in the most famous riff of their most famous song, the long instrumental jam that takes up most of "Light My Fire." A minute or so in, with Morrison having already sung a couple of verses, the song is handed over to Manzarek, who plays longer, increasingly more confident notes, painting arabesques with his Vox Continental, the scale going ever higher, true to the song's lyrics, before spiraling down again and into a release. Enter Robby Krieger and his Gibson SG, playing lazily, amusing himself with sliding scales, breaking between notes, throwing in the occasional pizzicato riff. John Densmore, meantime, is keeping the beat except for when he's not, and when he's out there pounding furiously, relieving unbearable urges, the rest of the band just plays along as if nothing has happened, waiting for him to rejoin them. This goes on for five minutes. Then they all replay the little phrase, that bit of carnival music, that got the song started, and Morrison joins in, announcing that the time to hesitate is through.

But Manzarek and Krieger and Densmore weren't really hesitating. There was no real resolution at the end of their journey, just repetition of the same verses Morrison had already sung. What they were doing was indulging themselves, each of them allowing himself to take his instrument as far as it would go, with little regard for the song as a cohesive unit. When "Light My Fire" came out, many DJs refused to play the song the whole way through. Fans of the Doors accused the DJs of boorishness, but the DJs were right: "Light My Fire" sounded less like a song and more like four guys giving musical monologues, each surrendering to his own excess. Writing about the song, Greil Marcus evoked the painter Manny

Farber's coinage, "termite art," which Farber explains as art that "feels its way through walls of particularization, with no sign that the artist has any object in mind other than eating away the immediate boundaries of his art, and turning these boundaries into conditions of the next achievement."[12] This kind of art, Marcus reasoned, is "art without intent, without thinking, art by desire, appetite, instinct, and impulse, and it can as easily meander in circles as cross borders and leap gaps."[13] It was art with no patience for tension. The fat boy who'd swallowed acid and woken up a rock god who could bed whomever he wanted made music that disdained seduction and concentrated on climax.

And he was not alone. The group of upstarts who released their debut albums in 1967—Jimi Hendrix, Janis Joplin, the Velvet Underground with Nico, Jefferson Airplane with Grace Slick—were similarly committed to challenging the conventions of rock and roll. Bright students of the art form's history, they'd learned from Chuck Berry that, in Robert Christgau's memorable phrase, "repetition without tedium is the backbone of rock 'n' roll."[14] But Berry—and, following him, most rock musicians up until 1966—kept his instrument in check, and played music that felt simultaneously dangerous (all that libidinal hip shaking!) and safe (all those pretty melodies!). This was the sort of equipoise that Nietzsche had in mind when he described art balanced between the Apollonian and the Dionysian, the former concerned with the sterile dictates of aesthetics and the latter with the lustful moans of arousal.

But the late 1960s were not years of measured response, and the rock stars who emerged to captivate charts and minds reveled, in true termite form, in destruction. Hendrix is the most obvious example: His control of the guitar and the effect pedals was absolute, and added deep layers of color and meaning to each note, but his chief signature was the Hendrix chord, the dominant seven-sharp ninth, which commands so many of his songs, most notably "Purple Haze." It's a jazzy chord, all internal friction, and other bands made use of it as well—listen for it in the Beatles' "Taxman"—but Hendrix electrified it, played it so loud and sure that it burst open and became a universe unto itself. The Hendrix chord, one writer noted, was essentially "the whole blues scale condensed into a single chord."[15] Joplin did something similar with her voice: In "Piece of My Heart," as the song nears its end, Joplin sings the chorus again and again and again before swallowing it up with a howl that makes it clear that the words are no longer important and that her enormous voice will now communicate solely by primal screams.

It wasn't a strategy that had any designs on longevity. Musical breakdowns may have been fascinating and liberating the first time you experienced them, but they posited the difficult question of what came next. If the Doors, say, were all about performance, about Morrison as trapeze artist[16] and Krieger, Densmore, and Manzarek as the world's most intricately porous safety net, what would they do for an encore? Launching into a meandering and aimless jam in "Light My Fire" before returning to the tune and its verses was one thing, but Morrison soon began asking what would happen if he didn't come back from the precipice, if he just kept on driving. Fueled by whiskey and hallucinogens, he wandered off beyond the songs. After being Maced backstage by a policeman who didn't recognize him, he took the stage, started singing, stopped, and ranted about the men in blue. A few of them soon came onstage and dragged him off. The crowd went wild. A riot, Morrison realized, is nothing but the best song that the Doors could never record; he made it his business to incite more. It was good for the whole rock-and-roll image, but it probably also felt right to a band that seemed to have come together only to come apart. And soon enough people started attending Doors concerts not as much to hear the music but to see what the wild man would do next.

Which drove the wild man wilder, first with joy and then with disdain. Whatever else Jim Morrison may have been, he was earnest and serious and believed deeply in his artistic experiment, and here were these people looking at him like an animal in the zoo, expecting him to amuse. During what is arguably the band's most notorious performance—the March 1, 1969, concert at the Dinner Key Auditorium in Miami, during which Morrison disrobed and either did or did not expose his penis, and which resulted in considerable legal and financial problems for him and the band—Morrison sang a few verses of "Five to One" and then raged at his fans. "You're all a bunch of fuckin' idiots," he bellowed. "Let people tell you what you're gonna do. Let people push you around. How long do you think it's gonna last? How long are you gonna let it go on? How long are you gonna let them push you around? Maybe you like it. . . . Maybe you love getting your face stuck in the shit. You're all a bunch of slaves. . . . What are you gonna do about it? What are you gonna do?"[17] And then he went back to singing, as if nothing had happened, before screaming that there were no rules, pretending to fellate Krieger, and setting off the frenzy that would lead to the show's implosion.

Two years, four months, and two days later, Morrison was dead. By then so were Joplin and Hendrix. All three died at twenty-seven. When their stories are told—and they are often told together—drugs receive pride of place, but their deaths were caused just as much by failure of the spirit as they were by depredations of the flesh. The three icons of the late 1960s died young because there was no other way for them to live: They piloted their own private cults in which release was paramount and delay, the cornerstone of faith, was rejected. They demanded transcendence without realizing that, attempted here on earth, it could lead only to demise.

With the culture seized by a death wish, Leonard Cohen grew ever more morose. Although he met the woman who would become the mother of his children, the teenage Suzanne Elrod, his reaction to events unfurling around him consisted of a series of rejections. First, in 1969, he turned down Canada's prestigious Governor General's Award, bestowed upon him for the anthology *Selected Poems: 1956–1968*. "Much in me strives for this honour," went his note, "but the poems themselves forbid it absolutely."[18] He did show up at a party his publisher, Jack McClelland, threw for the winners at the hotel Château Laurier in Ottawa, where he was cornered by Mordecai Richler. Visibly irate, Richler shoved Cohen into a bathroom. "C'mere," he snarled. "I want to talk to you." Then he closed the door, looked at Cohen, and demanded to know why Cohen had rejected the award. Cohen replied that he didn't know. "Any other answer," Richler said, "and I would have punched you in the nose."[19]

With Cohen's renown far greater in Europe than it was stateside, Columbia Records urged him to go on tour for the first time, which struck him as a bad idea; "the risks of humiliation," he told an interviewer years later, "were too wide."[20] Trying to find a creative way out of the constraint, he responded that he would only agree should Bob Johnston abandon his lucrative production work and join the tour as its manager and keyboard player, both being parts he had little experience playing. Johnston, who had recently terminated his contract with Columbia and was ready for a change of scene, agreed. In May 1970 he collected Cohen, a band of musicians, and copious amounts of hallucinogens, and off on tour they went.

Trouble brewed overnight. The tour's second performance, a May 4 concert at the Musikhalle in Hamburg, was about to begin when news came of the shootings at Kent State University, which left four dead and nine wounded. Stage fright, Mandrax, and political violence proved a heady cocktail. Cohen took the stage, played a few songs, then goose-stepped and Sieg Heiled. His outstretched arm drove the crowd mad. There was shouting. Some stormed the stage, which Cohen seemed to encourage. Someone thought someone had a gun. The police grew jittery. Peace was barely restored. Members of the band threatened to quit. None did, and Cohen's entourage, feeling more like a military unit than a band of touring musicians, became known as the Army.

Cohen, its commander, was on the attack. Everywhere he went, he challenged the local police. At the Olympia, Paris's celebrated concert hall, he urged the thousands in attendance to defy security and join him onstage. In Copenhagen he had them follow him back to his hotel. But if the local security guards were easy to overcome, the critics were less so. In London, Cohen sold out the Royal Albert Hall but failed to win over the press; his concerts, went the consensus, left "deep impressions of a sad and tortured wasteland."[21] New York was even worse: Playing in Forest Hills, Queens, Cohen left Nancy Erlich, a critic for *Billboard*, feeling disdainful. "He is a nervous and uncomfortable man," she wrote of the singer, "setting out to use his extraordinary command of language and of other people's emotions to make the rest of the world equally nervous and uncomfortable." Cohen's voice, Erlich wrote, was bloodless, dull, humorless, offering no comfort and no wisdom, expressing only defeat. "His art is oppressive," she concluded her assessment. "Rather than draw emotions out of his listeners, Cohen imposes his own, forcibly, through the pressure of his personality. There can be no catharsis when the communication does not work both ways."[22]

But if Cohen appeared uninterested in communicating with his listeners, his listeners sometimes seemed to return the favor. Everywhere from Venice Beach to Vienna, young men and women huddled together in what organizers billed as music festivals and expected something transcendent to happen. When it didn't, when nothing but men and women with guitars took the stage and admission fees were charged and sanitation was failing, they often curdled. Rock stars arrived at gig after gig to find themselves booed for being mere performers and not legislators, gurus, or prophets. Sometimes, as was the case on the Isle of Wight, it ended in arson. Sometimes, like the Rolling Stones concert at the free festival in Altamont, it ended in murder. Things were considerably calmer in Aix-en-Provence, but the same rancor was in the air: The naked people in the mud expected a revolution, and all they got was a lousy rock concert.

The Army realized the Aix festival would be trouble from the very drive up: The road leading to the bucolic field where the concert was to be held was blocked by dozens of cars, some having been abandoned by their owners, some occupied by irate and honking youth. It was the perfect visual representation of the festival's contentious mood, an ongoing skirmish between the organizers and the audience. On one side were Jean-Pierre Rawson, a noted Paris music impresario, and Claude Clément, a French army general who was forced to resign his post because of his association with the Organisation de l'armée secrète, a paramilitary group that opposed France's withdrawal from Algeria and tried to assassinate President Charles de Gaulle. His ultranationalist views aside, Clément was a patron of the arts and a member of the board of Aix-en-Provence's celebrated opera festival, and he believed that the hippies' love of music could, if cultivated, cure them of their boorish manners and their disdain for law and order. The local municipality was far from thrilled with the idea of throngs of young people, many of them still in the throes of the radical politics that had seized so many French students two years earlier, descending on the staid country town, but Clément had pull; he and Rawson, he promised, would produce a festival that would be to Woodstock what a fine baguette is to packaged sliced bread. The festival, its two producers announced, would be held on a seventy-five-acre lot of privately owned land, and would feature three open-air stages, twenty-two bands and solo artists, fifty hostesses, two hundred tents, a twenty-line telephone center, and mobile surgical and maternity units. All these amenities were expected to serve 150,000 concertgoers, each paying the steep price of fifty-five francs per ticket.[23]

Somewhere between seven and thirteen thousand people showed up. Clément's involvement had turned many cold to the festival, especially when someone started a rumor that the general had hired *harkis*—native Algerians who had fought on the French side during that country's war of independence—as security guards. Those who did try to make it to the festival's grounds were greeted by a massive police force that encircled the venue completely and made access a challenge and traffic unbearable. All this was too much for the young concertgoers to take. The festival, recalled rock critic Paul Alessandrini, felt like a "caricature of all that (and all those) which we refuse: recuperators who carry around with them the fetid odor of commerce, 'officials' who 'understand the problems of youth.'"[24] Even more vocal was a band of Maoists who had forced their way onto the grounds and demanded that the organizers forfeit the admission charge and turn the festival into a free public event. Clément refused, and, every bit the general, he stormed the stage and gave a stern speech, saying that the real youth had spoken and what the real youth wanted wasn't politics but rock and roll. Whether this was the case remained unknown, as the only voices audible throughout the festival's three-day run belonged to the Maoists, who yelled and did their best to shame the performers into stating support for their revolution.

As these small battles raged on, Leonard Cohen and the Army stood staring at a knot of automobiles. They were still far from the festival's site, and had heavy equipment with them. Walking was out of the question. A native of Hillsboro, Texas, Bob Johnston suggested horses. Some were procured from a stable nearby, and the Army rode on, stopping only for a prolonged visit to a nearby bar. Now fortified by drink,

Cohen decided to take the Western motif as far as it would go and ride onto the stage atop the white stallion he'd been assigned. The horse, angular, its golden mane flowing down to its midsection, looked regal; Cohen, his eyes glassy and his hair unkempt, looked confused.

As soon as Cohen and his steed mounted the stage, the booing began. To the young leftists seething on the grass, the rich Canadian entertainer riding a white horse was a grotesque display of might and arrogance. Those steeped in Cohen's biography shouted that he was a sympathizer of Greece's fascist regime—why else would a foreigner maintain a home on Hydra?—while the rest just demanded that he say something about ticket prices and condemn the bourgeoisie. Drunk, and most likely stoned, Cohen addressed the crowd. "I'd like to say something about the link between the festival and money," he said in his hesitant Québécois French. "When the festivals will be yours, they will not belong to others. If you call me, I will already be there. But the thing is, there is not a revolution. When others talk about the revolution, it is their revolution. Leave the revolution to the owners of the revolution. They are like any other owners. They're seeking profit." He was incoherent, but the message got through regardless: Talk of revolution was a sham, a fantasy that concealed the fact that earthly achievements required earthly labor and deserved earthly rewards, and that the people cultivating this fantasy were themselves, like everybody else, in it for fun and profit. Then he played "Bird on the Wire." The catcalls went on.

The politics, the police, and the frenzy exhausted Cohen. When the whole world was going mad, where did you go for shelter?

"I want to play mental asylums," Cohen told Bob Johnston.[25] The producer was no stranger to such requests; just two years earlier Johnny Cash had approached him with the task of arranging a gig at Folsom Prison. But Cash had intended for his prison concert to be recorded and released as an album. Cohen seemed drawn to asylums for entirely personal reasons. He never explained them to Johnston or to the other members of his band. Four years later, speaking to a reporter, he recalled his request and suggested that the "experience of a lot of people in mental hospitals would especially qualify them to be a receptive audience for my work."

In a sense," he continued, "when someone consents to go into a mental hospital or is committed he has already acknowledged a tremendous defeat. To put it another way, he has already made a choice. And it was my feeling that the elements to this choice, and the elements of this choice, and the elements of this defeat, corresponded with certain elements that produced my songs, and that there would be an empathy between the people who had this experience and the experience as documented in my songs."[26]

On August 28 the Army drove up to the Henderson Hospital, just south of London. "It was all talking therapy," a former nurse at the hospital told Cohen biographer Sylvie Simmons, "no medication, no 'zombies.'" Cohen was led up to the institution's imposing and narrow tower, where his impromptu performance would take place. "Oh boy," he told Johnston as they made their way in. "I hope they like 'So Long, Marianne.'" Most of those in attendance were young, and many were Leonard Cohen fans. The band quickly set up, and Cohen took his place at the front of the makeshift stage, underneath one of the "tall, narrow windows that gave the room the feel of a chapel."[27] He looked at the audience. "There was a fellow I spoke to last night," he said, "a doctor. I told him I was coming out here. He said, 'They are a tough bunch of young nuts.'" There was some applause, and Cohen started playing "Bird on the Wire." But then he stopped. "I feel like talking," he said. "Someone warned me downstairs that all you do here is talk. That's psychotic, it's contagious."

During eighty minutes, he played only eleven songs. The rest of the time he told the audience about his relationship with Marianne and how it had dissipated, about how "You Know Who I Am" was written after taking three hundred acid trips and "One of Us Cannot Be Wrong" was composed while coming down from amphetamine, about the Chelsea Hotel and life in New York and making love and sharing lovers and feeling inconsolably sad. Each time he finished a song or a speech, the audience applauded rapturously.

And then it was time to leave. "I really wanted to say that this is the audience that we've been looking for," Cohen said as the Army was packing up to go. "I've never felt so good playing before people."

"All Close Friends of the Artist, Please Leave"

few weeks after returning to the United States—the European tour ended with the August 31 concert on the Isle of
Wight—Cohen and the Army stepped into a Nashville studio
to record Cohen's third album. If *Songs from a Room* was slight
and melancholy, *Songs of Love and Hate* was dark and austere.
Most of its songs had been written while on tour, and they captured their author's mood perfectly. Cohen's old sensibility—
the one that could tell an intimate story that transformed, when
you thought about it, into (as a later song lyric so aptly put it)
"a manual for living with defeat"—had largely disappeared.
With the exception of "Famous Blue Raincoat," which struck
the familiar balance of the hopeful, the elegiac, the intimate,
and the eternal, the rest of the tracks are expeditions down
drill holes of despair. The opening track, "Avalanche," begins
with an ominous guitar, and then a violin, more ominous still,
joins in. Next comes Cohen, his voice flat, low, and devoid of its
usual warmth. If you were wondering what kind of an album
this was going to be, the first few lines left no doubt: "I stepped
into an avalanche / It covered up my soul."

It's a strange line. More than any other natural disaster, perhaps, an avalanche occurs rapidly and without warning, trapping everyone in its path, leaving little time or room for escape. But here was Cohen voluntarily walking into one—stepping, nonetheless, slowly and with deliberation—to the detriment of his spiritual well-being. Having lived for the first time the life of an entertainer, no longer privileged merely to release his albums and collect royalties in private, but obliged to meet his fans and their demands, Cohen contemplated the undertaking and found it a catastrophe. "When I am on a pedestal," he reflected in the same song, "You did not raise me there. / Your laws do not compel me / To kneel grotesque and bare. / I myself am the pedestal / For this ugly hump at which you stare." And if the trappings of renown were burdensome, they were also fleeting, like the old metaphysical Jewish joke about the food at a certain restaurant being not only bad but served in such small portions. By his third album and his fourth year as a singer, Cohen already felt, as he stated in the title of the album's second song, like "last year's man, / That's a Jew's harp on the table, that's a crayon in his hand. / And the corners of the blueprint are ruined since they rolled / Far past the stems of thumbtacks that still throw shadows on the wood / And the skylight is like skin for a drum I'll never mend / And all the rain falls down amen / On the works of last year's man." The symbolism hardly masks the autobiographical elements: Like the rest of the album, the song is a stark portrait of best-laid plans gone horribly wrong.

Something just as crushing had happened to Cohen's voice. Never a towering vocalist, he nevertheless managed, in his first two albums, to convey a considerable degree of warmth, his voice rising or dipping at key points in the delivery to create small wells of emotion and empathy. When he sings "Suzanne takes you down to her place near the river," for example, Cohen breaks the word "down" into two syllables, the first flat and the second low and mournful. But the woes of "Last Year's Man" receive no such nuanced styling. They're sung coldly, with little feeling. Two songs later, with "Diamonds in the Mine," Cohen goes a step further, channeling something that sounds like his inner Dylan: "The woman in blue," he sings, "she's asking for revenge, / The man in white (that's you) says he has no friends. / The river is swollen up with rusty cans / And the trees are burning in your promised land." The acerbic tone, the gnomic biblical allusions, the convoluted storytelling that conveys the mutterings of strange characters—the master from Hibbing couldn't have said it better himself. Cohen strains for that signature Dylan diction, stretching each word to its limit, and then lets his voice go growly for the chorus, sounding like a drunk at a hootenanny. A charitable listener could interpret his howls as a cry for help; a more exacting ear might spot something closer to a parody, as if the artist who had already abandoned two art forms was preparing to abandon a third. On the album's cover was a picture of Cohen's head, emerging from an otherwise uniformly dense pool of black, smiling, wild-eyed, looking not unlike Jack Nicholson in *One Flew Over the Cuckoo's Nest*. On the album's back runs a short poem: "They locked up a man / Who wanted to rule the world. The fools / They locked up the wrong man."

Songs of Love and Hate was a dismal failure in the United

States but was ecstatically received in Europe. In England critics were now calling Cohen "Laughing Len," and jokes abounded about his music being a sound track to suicide. He nonetheless appealed to large audiences, and Columbia pressured him into another promotional tour. In March 1972, with the Army by his side, Cohen returned to Europe.

For the first few nights things went smoothly.[1] The Army fell back into its old habits of drugs and camaraderie, and played Dublin and Glasgow without a hitch. Then something went wrong with the sound system. Someone argued it had to do with Bob Johnston sticking his earphones in the wrong jack and short-circuiting the entire setup of speakers and amps. Johnston denied it. But from day three of the tour, whenever the band picked up its instruments and started to play, all that many in the audience could hear was a crackle and an undulating pitch, like an alien spaceship attempting communication.

The whirs of the broken-down machines nicely matched Cohen's state of mind. In Berlin, after infuriating the audience by reciting a bit of a speech by Goebbels, Cohen greeted the noise by strumming on his guitar and breaking into an improvised song. "I don't know what to do about you, speaker," he sang to his broken-down equipment. "I suppose there's a solution, but it seems too drastic for me. But I'm going to be asking for the axe for the gun for the dynamite, and then just like the rest of the scene we'll just have to wait and see. Come on speaker, won't you speak to me? Come on speaker, let's just see what you've got to say, today." The audience laughed; Cohen didn't. Watching the concert footage, it's easy to wonder whether he's singing about a knot of wiring or about himself, a speaker grown weary of speaking.

The rest of the tour was dotted with similar moments, beginning with bursts of levity and ending with something more somber. When he took the stage in Manchester, the tour's third stop, Cohen had launched into a long digression. "It's like when Plato said," Cohen began, with the band playing what sounded like a sweet country ballad in the background. "No it wasn't," Jennifer Warnes and Donna Washburn, Cohen's backup singers, cooed softly. It was a well-timed gag. "It wasn't Plato," Cohen corrected himself as the audience giggled, "it was a cat that copied him, Socrates. I mean, Socrates didn't bother to write it down. But Plato saw he had a good gig writing it down. I'll write down everything he said, I'll publish it after he's dead. But all Socrates ever said was"—and here Cohen broke into song, the ballad finally coming to life—"no it wasn't any good, there's no reason why you should remember me." Speaking again, Cohen went on. "And I tell you, friends," he said, "you can tell this to your Sunday school teacher when she tells you about sin. This is the appropriate response." He waited a beat, then dived back into his song: "No it wasn't any good, there's no reason why you should remember me." Then the mood got darker. "You know that every word I say is being recorded and taken down on film," Cohen said. "And so no doubt, if electricity persists, and there are banks and governments devoted to its continuation, if electricity persists, perhaps our progeny, our grandchildren, in some new form of cool, in some new style of hip, in some new way of expansion, in some new trip on the old wine, perhaps they'll be able to see me standing here on this stage in Manchester which will then be a ruin—it's well on its way—and you know I hope the banks follow, and I hope the factories go down too, and I don't even like the places they live in here, and that's got nothing to do with the people, that's part of another scene. But anyhow, you know, I hope these imaginary descendants of mine would be able to look me straight in the screen, and I'll tell them one by one"—and he burst back into song—"No, it wasn't any good, there's no reason why you should remember me."

Were these the ramblings of a man in the throes of a mid-life crisis? Cohen was thirty-seven, and much of what he said publicly throughout the tour, to his audience or to the press, suggested a disconnect between the man who had written "Suzanne"—first as a poem and then as a song, while living in obscurity, walking the streets of Montreal, or swimming in the Aegean—and the man who was now forced to sing it night after night to tens of thousands of people who bobbed their heads and mouthed all the words reverentially. In Frankfurt, holding up a half-empty glass, he addressed the crowd, his eyelids heavy, his eyes glassy. "I see no reason why the energy has to be concentrated on this broken-down nightingale," he said, referring to himself. "I return it all to you, and if you could possibly make an evening out of this that is not just the observance and the documentation and the record of a few museum songs. After all, I wrote these songs to myself and to women several years ago, and it is a curious thing to be trapped in that original effort. I wanted to tell one person one thing, and now I am in a situation that I must repeat them like some parrot chained to his stand night after night." He made the same point more sharply a few days later, in an interview with British radio. "Sometimes you can live in a song," he said, "and sometimes it is inhospitable and it won't admit you and you're left banging at the door and everybody knows it. So it really depends a great deal on the moment, on the kind of shape you're in, on the kind of, on how straight you are with yourself at the moment, how straight you've been with the audience, many factors determine whether you're going to make the song live. There is another way a song can become inhospitable, in that you lose contact with the emotion of the song after you've been singing a song that perhaps you wrote six or seven years ago and you've sung it like maybe ten or fifteen times in a row, each night in a different city, you lose contact with the song itself." The radio reporter nodded politely, and thanked Cohen for his patience. Then, running back the tape to check the sound quality, he realized he'd forgotten to press Record.

But there was more plaguing Cohen than faulty equipment and the vagaries of fame. The documentary filmmaker Tony Palmer accompanied Cohen on the tour and captured a man paralyzed by what seemed to be a case of existential jitters. It's not difficult to guess why: If the 1970 tour was marred by recurrent interruptions from ideologues seized by the spirit of revolution, the 1972 tour featured mostly content young men and women, enraged only by the feeling of not having gotten their money's worth on account of the bad speakers. The closest Cohen came to confronting his fans was in Stockholm, when a few bespectacled men slinked backstage, accused Cohen of behaving unprofessionally, and refused to leave until the singer pulled out some crumpled wads of cash from his own pocket and offered them by way of compensation. It was a far cry from the Maoists in Aix or the rowdy bunch on the hill on the Isle of Wight. In the course of just two or three years, it seemed, the youth themselves had changed.

The music had, too. In 1969, for example, Billboard's top ten chart was dominated by the Beatles and the Rolling Stones, by the 5th Dimension announcing a new cosmic age in "Aquarius" and Sly and the Family Stone pleading for racial harmony in "Everyday People." In 1972, the songs topping the same chart were Roberta Flack's "The First Time Ever I Saw Your Face," Gilbert O'Sullivan's "Alone Again," Harry Nilsson's "Without You," and other sweet confections of sentimental love. Even worse, the baton of serious rock and roll had been passed from the solemn seekers—the Morrisons and Wilsons and Joplins—to the excessive thinkers and tinkerers, men like Keith Emerson and Jon Anderson and Roger Waters, fathers of the new style known as progressive rock.

It is hard to think of rock and imagine a more natural progression than the one that led from the Beach Boys and the Doors to the Nice, Emerson's first, influential band, or to Anderson's Yes. All shared the same goal: "discovery of the self and connection with the divine,"[2] as Anderson recently put it in an interview. But whereas the rockers of the 1960s cast their gaze Eastward in the hope of finding spiritual inspiration, the rockers of the 1970s looked backward to a past half real and half imagined, evoking a bestiary of mythical creatures in their songs and on their album covers. Curiously, this approach did not translate into similarly pagan sounds. To the contrary: The new cadre of musicians did not so much feel or trip their way into their songs as they thought their music through, which explains the abundance of concept albums rich with movements and themes. The Nice's second album, for example, was called *Ars Longa Vita Brevis*. Released in 1968, it was influenced by the assassination of Robert F. Kennedy, an event that inspired Keith Emerson to have the highly unoriginal thought that gives the album its title. Should the Latin have failed to convey that this was a magnum opus to be consumed with the utmost reverence, and should fans have failed to be awed by the album's cover—an X-ray of the band's members that, due to their having ingested radioactive substances, glowed in orange and purple and green—Emerson included a short message on the album's sleeve: "Newton's first law of motion states a body will remain at rest or continue with uniform motion in a straight line unless acted on by a force," it begins. "This time the force happened to come from a European source. Ours is an extension of the original Allegro from Brandenburg Concerto No. 3. Yesterday I met someone who changed my life, today we put down a sound that made our aim accurate. Tomorrow is yesterday's history and art will still be there, even if life terminates." Peter Sinfield, who wrote most of Emerson's lyrics when the latter joined with Greg Lake and Carl Palmer, had it just right when he quipped that prog rock was the domain of "small people with big ideas."[3]

Whatever else these ideas were about, they were predominantly about sound, and the extent to which instruments could be tortured to produce strange and alarming sounds. If Ray Manzarek squeezed his keyboard in search of a feeling,

Emerson stabbed his with a knife for no other reason than to make it cry. After being X-rayed for the cover of *Ars Longa*, Emerson learned that three of his ribs were broken. "You break ribs playing keyboards?" his doctor wondered. "I wouldn't have considered it such a hazardous occupation." Emerson replied that it depended on how one played them.[4] Soon enough the equipment eclipsed the musicians, as stories about prog rock icons inevitably began with fawning accounts of the complexity of their machinery. When Emerson, Lake & Palmer played New York in 1973, for example, the *New York Times* began its report of the upcoming concerts with what read more like a roadie's checklist than a reporter's attempt at insight: Emerson, Lake & Palmer, went the article, "is due at Madison Square Garden tomorrow and Tuesday with over 200 separate items of equipment, valued by Customs at just over $100,000. The equipment ranges from the sublime—a brand new prototype Moog synthesizer, one of the 13 keyboard units used by Keith Emerson, who started out, he says, 'as a laid back piano player'—to Item 107 on Emerson, Lake and Palmer's list, a Persian carpet. The carpet is for bass player Greg Lake to stand on while playing and is reputed to have cost around $5,000." And then it was on to describing Palmer's drum set, topped by an old church bell "from the Stepney district of London."[5] Emerson himself was happy to comment on this line of inquiry. Speaking mainly in proper nouns, he extolled the virtues of his Hammond and his Moog and the rest of what he referred to as "rock technology." Thirteen keyboards, he told the reporter, was about what it took just to get a song across. "It is very hard to get something across to 10,000 people with just a piano, a bass and a set of drums."[6]

Leonard Cohen, of course, disagreed. He had gotten more across to more people with much less instrumentation than the big bands were now lugging around. His audience, however, had always been comprised of smart and sensitive young people, and, in 1972, smart and sensitive young people everywhere believed that the proper venue in which to be moved by music was the arena, and that songs approached their apotheosis the lengthier they were and the more they changed time signatures. David Weigel summed up the period elegantly when he explained that "Rick Wakeman could write a thematic micro-opera about the Knights of the Round Table, and sell 10 million copies. In 14 months, Jethro Tull recorded not one but two albums that consisted of single, 40-minute songs. And they *both went platinum*."[7]

None of Cohen's albums to that point had sold as well, and he continued his tour, his speakers screeching and his faith shaken. Audiences seemed to baffle him. In Frankfurt he became visibly annoyed by repeated shouts requesting one song or another. It's a common enough occurrence in a rock concert—the charming and hopeless attempts of many in the crowd to communicate with the musician onstage—but Cohen was unamused. "Would you please appoint a spokesman?" he chastised his audience with uncharacteristic humorlessness. Of course they didn't, and when the shouting continued Cohen's tone grew more severe. "Anyone else got anything to say?" he asked curtly, picking nervously at his guitar. "I can stand here for a long time like this. I'm tough, you know. I can take this." The shouting eventually died down. Cohen smiled. "Nice and quiet now, eh?" he said. Later on that evening, after leaving the stage, he admitted that his behavior had been disgraceful.

It was not, however, uncommon. He played a few notes in Copenhagen, and when the audience applauded he said, smiling but visibly irate, "Now listen, you couldn't possibly know what song it is." The audience applauded louder yet. "I start all my songs that way," Cohen continued. "It's the only chord I know." A fan shouted from the floor, "Sing it anyway! They're all wonderful songs!" Cohen's expression changed. "Oh, thank you," he said, looking meek. "Forgive my ingratitude. Really, oh, forgive me. It's the first day of Passover, and I'm, I'm . . ." Someone shouted and informed Cohen that it was the holiday's last day, not the first. "The last one," Cohen agreed. "You see, that's how confused I am. It's the festival of freedom, and I'm trying to break free myself." And then he started howling an improvised song: "I'm trying to break free myself, you know / Trying to lose my old songs / Trying to start a new life before it is too late / Trying to get along / Trying to get along / Trying to get along."

On April 19 the tour landed at Ben Gurion Airport in Israel for two final concerts, one that evening in Tel Aviv and another two days later in Jerusalem. Cohen's Army had had a turbulent month, and the musicians hoped that a few days in Israel would prove rewarding. Cohen was thrilled to see Jerusalem, subject of so much Jewish prayer, and knew that his songs, with their occasional biblical allusions, were particularly popular in Israel. He entered the Yad Eliyahu sports arena, a gray concrete monstrosity in an impoverished neighborhood in the south of Tel Aviv, with high expectations. All, however, were dashed when he learned that the concert's organizers had set up a security perimeter covering the arena's entire floor, barring anyone from getting near the stage. Fans were confined to their seats, which were far off to the side and offered compromised vision and sound.

Cohen, infuriated by the setup, called on his audience to come closer. A phalanx of guards in orange shirts tried to keep the fans from approaching the stage. In audio recordings of that evening, fists whiz audibly through the air. Fans rushed the stage, some grabbing instruments. Musicians were hit. True to his designation as the Army's commander in chief, Cohen ordered retreat. A few minutes later, he marched the band back onstage. "I'd like to sing this song for the men in orange," he said, nodding at the guards. "I know you guys are doing your work. Why don't you just sit down and enjoy the concert?" And then he invited the audience to come on down once more, carried on for a few more songs, and then played "Passing Through," a melancholy country tune in which Jesus, Adam, George Washington, and FDR all make wry remarks on the transient nature of life. The Army's musicians were standing close together, arranged in a tight circle, looking more like a group of friends huddling for warmth than like a band playing for tens of thousands of fans. The audience, however, was still not calm, and after singing the song's chorus six or seven times, Cohen realized it was time to leave. "Let's not go that way," he said. "Let's just do our own scene, disperse quietly, and let's just take off, be together somewhere else. Because this scene isn't working. So I just want to say good night to you, just passing by, I just want to say good night. There's no point starting a war right now."

With such havoc marring their first concert in Israel, the

band feared the second would turn out to be just as disastrous. It did. Jerusalem's Binyanei Ha'Uma convention center offered terrific acoustics, and the audience was giddy, but Cohen himself was under a dark cloud. Earlier that morning, when a reporter asked if he was a practicing Jew, Cohen sounded somber. "I'm always practicing," he said. "Sometimes, I feel the fear of God. I do feel that fear sometimes. I got to get myself together. I don't know whether it's an exclusively Jewish phenomenon, but it's certainly one that is part of the Jewish strain, to sensitize yourself to that kind of direction." He sang a few songs, and they were greeted with wild applause, but Cohen felt that his delivery was cold and deadened. "You don't want to go in front of people unless you feel that you can give them something, and you can return to them the love that they feel to you through your songs," he said in an interview a few days earlier. "When you don't feel that you can make it, it's a terrible feeling. You feel that you are cheating people."

"If it doesn't get any better," he told the audience, "we'll just end the concert and I'll refund your money. Some nights, one is raised off the ground, and some nights you just can't get off the ground. There's no point lying about it. And tonight we just haven't been getting off the ground. It says in the kabbalah that if you can't get off the ground, you should stay on the ground. It says in the kabbalah that unless Adam and Eve face each other, God does not sit on his throne. Somehow the male and female parts of me refused to encounter one another tonight, and God does not sit on his throne. And this is a terrible thing to happen in Jerusalem. So listen, we're going to leave the stage now, and try to profoundly meditate in the dressing room, to get ourselves back into shape. And if we can manage, we'll be back."

Back in the dressing room, Cohen was in a daze. "I can't make it, man," he said, smiling nervously. "I don't like it. I'm splitting." He got up, but he didn't go anywhere. He had sent his manager, Martin Machat, to see if the audience would accept refunds, and soon Machat returned and reported that the audience wouldn't budge. A few young men, he said, had told him that they didn't even care if Cohen sang or not; they loved him so much, they just wanted him on the stage, and they would sing to him. Many in the audience had the same idea: From the dressing room Cohen could hear the hall rattled by thousands of people singing "Hevenu Shalom Aleichem," a popular folk song whose one-line lyric means "We have brought peace upon you." Cohen calmed down a bit. He sank into a chair, still saying that he didn't want to go back out. Someone was telling him that maybe some of his Israeli fans didn't want to be soldiers and shoot people, but that they had to do it anyway, just like he had to reclaim the stage and finish the concert.

Cohen listened silently, his face buried in a bouquet of roses someone had handed him. Suddenly he shot to his feet. "Oh, I know what I have to do," he said. "I have to shave." He walked over to the sink, produced a small shaving kit, and turned on the warm water. "What a life," he said repeatedly as he rid himself of his stubble, "what a life. This is wonderful." Bob Johnston, Ron Cornelius, and the other members of the Army stood behind him, laughing. Cohen, too, looked like a man emerging from a long and terrifying trip. "Oh, this is really great," he exclaimed, finishing at the sink. "Oh, this gig ain't over, oh no." He brought the razor to his wrist, and made a mock slashing motion. Johnston and Cornelius cracked up. Cohen dried his face, sat down again, and smoked a cigarette. He was still not sure if he wanted to go back out, but his mood was different. "Bombed in Jerusalem," he quipped, and then, turning serious, leaned in. "I felt this atmosphere once before," he said. "It was in Montreal. My entire family was there. Their cousins, aunts, daughters, and nieces. I'm going to ask everybody from Montreal to leave. Just the people from Montreal will get their money back. All close friends of the artist, please leave."

And with that, it was back out and onto the stage. The audience, still singing "Hevenu Shalom Aleichem," sang louder, clapping wildly. Cohen just stood there, his arms folded and resting on his guitar. Then he played "Hey, That's No Way to Say Goodbye" and "So Long, Marianne," and the audience applauded more fiercely, more reverentially than Cohen or his musicians had ever heard any audience applaud before. It was overwhelming.

Backstage, Jennifer Warnes and Donna Washburn were weeping, hugging each other for support. Cohen was weeping, too. He told Bob Johnston that he couldn't go back out there and cry in front of all these people. Johnston said they wouldn't leave. They needed another encore. But Cohen didn't have another song in him. He stepped back out and grabbed the microphone with both hands. "Hey listen, people, my band and I are all crying backstage there. We're too broken up to go on, but I just wanted to tell you thank you, and good night." Amid the sound of a thousand gasps and yelps, he made his way backstage again, sat down, lit another cigarette. "What an audience," he said to no one in particular. "Ever see anything like that?" And then, once again, he started to cry.

CHAPTER EIGHT

"There Is a War"

The war broke out on October 6, 1973. Israelis should have seen it coming: The Egyptians had been moving their troops to the border for days, and there were indications that the Syrians, too, were preparing for battle. King Hussein of Jordan secretly flew to Tel Aviv and told Prime Minister Golda Meir that she had days, maybe less, before an assault began. But too many Israeli officials refused to believe it would happen; Egypt and Syria were just flexing their muscles, they argued, and wouldn't dare risk another military defeat like the one they were dealt in 1967. It was Yom Kippur, Judaism's holiest day, and most Israelis, secular and religious alike, spent it fasting and praying in the synagogues. It was there that they heard the sirens, and soon after them the roar of military jeeps rushing to the front, or, rather, fronts: Egypt had invaded from the south, Syria from the north, each country fortified by soldiers from a host of other Arab nations. The invaders were met by a smattering of young soldiers, terrified and overwhelmed, desperate for reinforcement. Because almost every Israeli served in the army, and because nearly all continued to serve for a month or two a year in reserve duty until they were well into middle age, the Israeli Defense Forces' doctrine specified that in case of a surprise attack, all the conscripts had to do was hold the line until the older, more experienced veterans got there. On October 6 that meant that nearly all Israeli men younger than fifty-five were en route to war.

The artists would be on their way, too: In cafés all over Tel Aviv, singers, actors, and musicians gathered in haste to plan impromptu tours of the front lines, eager to provide a few hours of entertainment to the men fighting and dying there. In Pinati, one such café, Oshik Levi, a handsome pop star whose second album had come out earlier that year, presided over one such gathering. With him were Ilana Rovina, a chanteuse and the daughter of the legendary theater actress Hannah Rovina; the singer and actor Pupik Arnon; and a young musician named Mati Caspi, who would soon become one of Israel's most iconic singer-songwriters but was still, at the time, a quirky kid with sad eyes.[1] They were putting together a show they would soon take to various air bases, where wounded soldiers, airlifted from makeshift hospitals up front, were laid on tarmacs before being taken to proper clinics for treatment.

At the other end of the café Levi spotted a thin man sitting by himself. He seemed vaguely familiar, and Levi, half joking, told his friends that the man looked a little bit like Leonard Cohen. "Don't you wish!" said Rovina. Like most Israelis, they were all fans of Cohen. The odds that the same man who had caused such a sensation in his shows in Tel Aviv and Jerusalem just a year earlier would now be sitting there at their café, unannounced and unaccompanied, in the middle of a war, seemed very slim. Still, they couldn't look away. A few moments later, Levi spoke again. "I swear on my life," he said.

"It's Leonard Cohen." He got up and walked over to the thin stranger. "Are you Leonard Cohen?" he asked. The man said, "I am."

It was a dreamlike moment for Levi, improbable and a touch surreal. As in a dream, he understood that the situation had its own logic. Coolly he invited Cohen to his table, and there, without thinking about it too much, told Cohen about the upcoming tour and asked him if he'd like to join.

Cohen seemed confused. He had come to Israel just the day before, he said, boarding a boat from Hydra to Athens and then flying into Tel Aviv as soon as he heard news of the attack. He left behind his wife, Suzanne, and a year-old son, Adam, but he couldn't stay away. He had no idea why, or what he would do once he arrived. Maybe, he told his new friends, he should move to a kibbutz and help out with the crops. Levi said that entertaining the troops would be a much bigger service, and Cohen, intrigued, replied that he would like to but had left in haste and did not bring his guitar. Rushing to a nearby phone, Levi called a senior air force officer and secured a guitar for Cohen. The tour left Tel Aviv that same night, its first stop being the southern air force base in Hatzor.

During the drive Cohen had his doubts; his songs, he told Levi, were sad, hardly the sort of stuff designed to boost the morale of fighting men. Levi replied that it didn't matter, that just seeing the star there with them in the middle of the war would do wonders for the soldiers' morale. They arrived at the base, and Levi took the small makeshift stage. He introduced his friends, and then paused for a beat and said that he was happy to announce a very special guest performer, Leonard Cohen. At first no one clapped. No one believed him. The silence persisted when Cohen stepped out, blinking at the bright spotlights flashing in his eyes. Then rapture—a throng of exhausted soldiers howling and clapping wildly.

After years of growing anxiety and creeping despair and songs that got bleaker and more caustic, something in Cohen was transformed. As soon as he stepped off the stage, he took his guitar and wrote a new song, "Lover, Lover, Lover." He played a version of it in his second performance, later that night. Something about the desert and the instruments of war inspired the song's rolling beats and lyrics. "And may the spirit of this song," Cohen sang. "May it rise up pure and free. / May it be a shield for you, / A shield against the enemy." The same spirit guided Cohen in the days and weeks that followed. In some outposts he played standing up, with a soldier holding a flashlight and making Cohen's face just barely visible. Often, he, Levi, and the others would simply drive along the front lines, stopping whenever they saw a handful of soldiers and surprising them with a few tunes. It wasn't uncommon for the soldiers to clap along enthusiastically, wait until the end of the song, load and fire their small cannons at the Egyptian soldiers invisible in the distance, and then sit back down to hear another song. Here, finally, was a dynamic between a performer and an audience that Cohen could tolerate, even embrace. In one concert, in Sinai, performing for paratroopers who were a few hours away from flying into battle, he asked the men to huddle around him, and then started strumming the first bars of "So Long, Marianne." The song, he told his khaki-clad audience of a few dozen fatigued men, "was meant to be listened to at home, with one hand holding a drink and the other embracing a beloved woman. May you all soon find yourselves in that condition."[2] He kept this regimen, performing four, five, even eight times a day for nearly three months. "War," he told an interviewer the following year, "is wonderful. They'll never stamp it out. It's one of the few times people can act their best. It's so economical in terms of gesture and motion, every single gesture is precise, every effort is at its maximum. Nobody goofs off. Everybody is responsible for his brother. The sense of community and kinship and brotherhood, devotion. There are opportunities to feel things that you simply cannot feel in modern city life. Very impressive."[3]

It's easy to dismiss such statements as the glib pronouncements of a thrill-seeking dilettante, as Cohen's brother-in-law had done upon the poet's return from Cuba. The purity of war, after all, had been a constant theme for many writers with a utopian streak, especially ones who, like Cohen, grew up in households governed by the mystique of military life. But Cohen's wartime clarity was far greater than his statement let on. He wasn't just playing at being a Hemingway manqué, a good man seeking solace in some prelapsarian heaven where absolute good fights absolute evil and where men transcend all pettiness to form eternal bonds forged by fire. His vision was far more complex. He expressed it a few years later in an interview with filmmaker Harry Raskay. "Even in the midst," he said, his words stumbling as he sought to capture the idea, "in the midst of this flood, or catastrophe which we are in, these are the days of the flood, these are the final days, in a sense, all these institutions are and have been swept away. And the ethical question is what is the proper behavior, what is the appropriate behavior in the midst of a catastrophe, in the midst of a flood."[4] This is what the war had given Cohen—removed from fame and expectations, his relationship with the young mother of his child rocky, he experimented in the desert with new ideas about living in a shattered world. He was no longer Laughing Len, recorder of woes, a mood ring getting progressively darker. Being in an actual existential crisis—a nation fighting for its survival—made the metaphorical existential crisis, the one he had grappled with for so long, the one at the heart of the modern experience, that much easier to understand. In the desert Cohen had begun working on his next album, and it would sound nothing like the previous three.

Not that John Lissauer would have known: When he met Cohen, the music producer, then twenty-three, had heard about Montreal's most famous singing son, but very little of his actual work. Lissauer, a native New Yorker, was in Canada to produce a record for Lewis Furey, a bisexual avant-garde actor and musician. It suited his sensibility as a college-educated composer, jazz musician, and lover of serious challenging music. He associated Cohen with folk music, and thought folk music to be largely uninteresting, the refuge of guitar players who couldn't really play guitar. But Cohen, who approached him after a Furey concert one night, was exceedingly polite and somewhat well known, and when he asked to come see Lissauer in New York, the young producer happily extended an invitation.

A few weeks later Cohen arrived. Lissauer was living in a loft on Eighteenth Street. He tossed the key out the window for Cohen to let himself in. Walking up the stairs, Cohen came across a pizza delivery man who happened to be headed to the same floor. The singer, always the gentleman, paid for the pizza and carried the box upstairs. He knocked on the door of the apartment across the hall from Lissauer's, which happened to be occupied by a rabid Cohen fan. Its tenant opened the door, saw her idol holding her lunch, and began to shriek.

Watching all this from his apartment door, Lissauer smiled. By then he had heard Cohen's previous albums, and was delighted to learn that the artist known for his gloomy music was a warm and playful man. "The guy," Lissauer recalled observing, "has his twinkly side."[5] Cohen walked in and played Lissauer three songs: "Lover, Lover, Lover," "Chelsea Hotel," and "There Is a War." The last one had its roots in the Sinai Desert, although the war it described wasn't between Israel and a coalition of Arab nations but between the rich and the poor, the left and the right, the odd and the even, the women and the men. It began with Cohen's signature style of strumming, rapid and urgent, but levity was soon introduced into both the music and the words. "Why don't you come on back to the war, don't be a tourist," Cohen crooned, his voice going as high as it could, sounding merry and defiant. Then an outright declaration of transformation: "You cannot stand what I've become, / You much prefer the gentleman I was before. / I was so easy to defeat, I was so easy to control, / I didn't even know there was a war." This, Lissauer thought, was a departure from Cohen's earlier, "severely black-suited" stuff. Here was Cohen, amused and defiant, ready for a new sound. Lissauer was ready for one, too.

"I thought pop music was, for the most part, predictable and unexplorative," Lissauer said. "It didn't reach out, it didn't do half of the things I thought it was going to do after the Beatles, after the Stones, when they were really using everything. I said this is great, this is going to open it up, this rather limited rock n' roll world which is somewhat four-chordish and has very limited instrumentation. The Beatles started stretching out, and then 1970 happened and it was wham, right back to the same seven instruments, guitar, bass, drums, piano, maybe some organ, a little bit of percussion. I wanted it to get colorful."

When he and Cohen entered the studio, Lissauer borrowed a collection of uncommon instruments from an acquaintance, a musician who played with the New York Philharmonic. "There Is a War" now began with African percussion instruments chasing the guitar into the song, giving the otherwise flat melody a depth that suggested tribal rites and rituals. By the time Cohen hit the refrain about coming back to the war, strings played wryly in the background for short and declarative musical phrases that seemed to egg the singer on, to urge him back into combat. Cohen had recorded more beautiful songs before, and more memorable ones, but they were all delicate creatures supported by the twin frail skeletons of an elemental melody and haunting lyrics. Songs like "Suzanne" or "Sisters of Mercy" were tightly knit creations, almost too perfect to live in this world; they worked as pieces of music because they enchanted listeners away from reality, inviting them to take shelter in the walled gardens of their ethereal beauty. But "There Is a War" was different. It was a song of this world, earthy and funny and angry. The prophet Cohen was coming down from the mountaintop.

The same thing happened on nearly every other song in the album. "Field Commander Cohen," for example, began with a monotone lament of having abandoned thrills such as "parachuting acid into diplomatic cocktail parties" for the banalities of everyday life, a parade of "silver bullet suicides, / and messianic ocean tides, / and racial roller-coaster rides / and other forms of boredom advertised as poetry." Then comes a tender moment—the singer gently chiding himself by saying that even though life is hard, "many men are falling where you promised to stand guard"—but the song isn't content to remain mute or solemn. It creeps toward a triumphalist mood, with ever-louder strings surging in the background and Cohen, thawing, referring to himself with a wink as "the patron saint of envy and the grocer of despair." Finally, just in case anyone didn't get the joke, he riffs on the Andrews Sisters and sings that he's "working for the Yankee dollar."[6] Even "Who by Fire," the album's most somber composition—which Cohen based on the Unettaneh Tokef, a Jewish liturgical poem that is recited on Yom Kippur—was redeemed from its own innate darkness by two elements. First, after paraphrasing the prayer's recitation of the various ways in which those who have displeased the Lord might find their end—avalanche, barbiturates, hunger—Cohen added the line, "And who shall I say is calling?" The prayer concludes differently: After counting the ways in which the Almighty may smite his subjects, it comforts by reminding us mortals that "repentance, prayer, and charity avert the severe decree." Cohen, however, remained defiant. Rather than prostrate himself before the Lord—the purpose of the Yom Kippur service in which the prayer is read and in which Jews ask God to forgive them their sins—Cohen coolly reacted to the divine decrees as if they were nothing more than a phone call from a stranger, meriting distance and a hint of suspicion.

He wasn't just being defiant. He was channeling one of Judaism's core traditions, which held that despite their divine origin, God's decrees were not exempt from human scrutiny.

A Talmudic tale illustrates this point nicely. It tells of a group of rabbis engaged in a discussion about the meaning of a particular ritual. One of them, Eliezer, holds a divergent view. Eager to demonstrate to the others that he's in the right, Eliezer calls on a nearby tree to provide proof. Miraculously the tree leaps in the air and lands a few feet away. But the other rabbis aren't impressed. A tree, they say, doesn't prove anything. Frustrated, Eliezer points to a succession of inanimate objects, all of which perform extraordinary feats: Walls tremble, water flows backward, and other natural orders are reversed. Still, the rabbis remain unmoved. Enraged, Eliezer calls on God himself to intervene, and the Lord speaks and states, in a voice loud and clear, that Eliezer was correct and the other rabbis wrong. This, too, fails to move them. The discussion, they tell God, was being held on earth, not in heaven, and his voice, therefore, held no special sway. The story ends with a report that not long after these events took place, one of the men happened upon the prophet Elijah, who reported that when God was rebuked by the rabbis, he laughed with joy and shouted happily, "My children have defeated me!"[7]

Cohen's quip, though subtle, showed the same kind of mirthful disregard for divine authority. Before he succumbed to any grim fate, the singer wanted to know just who was doing the judging. To underscore that spirit, Lissauer wanted the song's arrangement to veer toward the "avant-garde pagan." As it draws to its end, all those strings and strange percussion tools he'd used throughout the album come in for a short, fierce, and disjointed moment that lasts about half a minute and serves to scrub the song of its liturgical evocations. We can pray for mercy all we want, the song's final segment tells us, but that won't change the fact that we are alone and alienated, more likely to condemn one another to death than to support one another in life. The original prayer offers the comfort of community and religion; Cohen's song took it away and replaced it with the dry, terrifying wit of a single phrase: "Who shall I say is calling?"

The album, however, owed its mordant tone to more than its author's theological reflections. His relationship with Suzanne was rocky. Despite her being the mother of his son, the two never married, a decision Cohen, speaking to an interviewer decades later, attributed simply to "cowardice"[8] on his part. Cohen tried to leave: As he crooned in one of the album's most beautiful tracks, "I don't deny / I tried to close the book on us, at least a hundred times. / I'd wake up every morning by your side." The song neatly captures the sweet sorrow of an impossible relationship that allows neither resolution nor closure. Playing something that sounds like a blues chord slowly melting in the heat, Cohen sings apathetically, his voice like molasses. You needn't know much about the singer's personal life to realize that he's stuck and trying to sing his way out of a stalemate.

To the extent that the mainstream music press cared about Leonard Cohen in 1974, the record was well received, with nearly all critics noting the change in tone and texture. But once again,Cohen was a man out of sync with his time: Two artistic forces were busy being born that year, and none had much room for a singer-songwriter with heavenly obsessions.

The first was punk. On March 30, in New York City, the Ramones, then still a trio, took the stage for the very first time. Their set was short and declarative; the songs all had titles like "I Don't Wanna Go Down to the Basement," "I Don't Like Nobody That Don't Like Me," and "Now I Wanna Sniff Some Glue." If the lyrics did not suffice to convey the spirit of the new genre, the music did—a few chords, played fast and furiously, the words howled, the sound dirty. A few months later, in June, Patti Smith recorded her first single, a cover of Jimi Hendrix's "Hey Joe." Blondie, the Talking Heads, and the Stranglers all formed in 1974.

On the other end of the musical divide were the maximalists. In April, Queen played its first North American gig. It was supported by its first big American hit, "Killer Queen," a lush and symphonic arrangement that offered a candy store's worth of vocal harmonies, études, and other beautiful sonorities. David Bowie was still performing as Ziggy Stardust, his face-painted cult-leader alter ego. And slightly to the right, their sound harder but their gestalt every bit as glamorous and showy, were new acts like Kiss, Van Halen, Cheap Trick, and Alice Cooper. As the seventies hurtled toward its end, these trends intensified: To succeed, artists had to sound either very big or very small.

Cohen, as usual, was in the middle. And his manager, Martin Machat, was painfully aware of that fact. His artist, Machat believed, was long overdue for a breakout hit, a record that would put him up there with Elton John, Billy Joel, and the decade's other rising stars. It was time, Machat believed, to stop working with kids like Lissauer, young and artistically minded. If Cohen wanted a hit, he had to collaborate with someone who knew how to make one.

Someone like Phil Spector. The legendary record producer, another one of Machat's clients, had started off the decade well.

After a brief reclusive period in the late 1960s, he reemerged to assert his claim on the sound of pop, producing *Let It Be* for the Beatles, *Imagine* for John Lennon, and George Harrison's masterpiece, *All Things Must Pass*. In March 1974, however, he crashed his car in Hollywood, flew through the windshield, hit the ground, and was so badly hurt he required nearly a thousand stitches to his head and face. To cover his disfigurement, he began wearing wigs. To cope with the trauma, his behavior became more erratic than ever. When he first invited Leonard Cohen and Suzanne for dinner in his house, he flew into a rage when the couple, tired after a long meal, got up to leave, and ordered his servants to lock the doors.[9] The Cohens remained seated, surrounded by Spector's armed guards, imprisoned in the producer's dimly lit mansion. They were freed only in the morning.

Spector's insanity aside, there were many other plausible reasons why Cohen should not have collaborated with him. The latter was, in Tom Wolfe's memorable phrase, "the first tycoon of teen," the man who piled up the ooh-las to create scores of hits for the young and the restless; the former was the sort of artist who sought inspiration in liturgy. And Cohen's albums, his most recent being the exception, were spare, while Spector's approach to record production was known as the Wall of Sound, in which brigades of musicians battled in the studio and delighted in hearing their notes bleed into one another to create an overwhelming musical totality. Cohen and Spector, however, shared not only a manager but also an infatuation with popular music in all its varieties, and an obsession with the intricacies of the songwriting process. To that end a partnership was proposed: Cohen would write the words, Spector the music. Each man would be relieved of his weakness and allowed to concentrate on his true passion.

The two began working in earnest, often spending entire nights in Spector's home. Cohen noted the eccentricities of his new partner—it was impossible not to—but enjoyed the process nonetheless. "He really is a magnificent eccentric," he said of Spector in an interview some years later. "And to work with him just by himself is a real delight. We wrote some songs for an album over a space of a few months. When I visited him we'd have really good times and work till late in the morning. But when he got into the studio he moved into a different gear, he became very exhibitionist and very mad."[10]

His madness was evident at first sight. As Cohen entered the studio in January 1977 to begin recording the new album, he saw "a room crammed with people, instruments and microphone stands. There was barely space to move. He counted forty musicians, including two drummers, assorted percussionists, half a dozen guitarists, a horn section, a handful of female backing singers and a flock of keyboard players."[11]

Orchestrating this cacophony was Spector, standing behind his console, screaming, ordering people to do exactly as he said. Bob Dylan and Allen Ginsberg, who were brought in to sing background vocals on "Don't Go Home with Your Hard On," weren't spared. Listening to his playback, Spector played the music so loudly that he caused the speakers to explode and had to relocate the entire session to another studio. He was perpetually drunk and never unarmed; others in the studio, including the bodyguards Spector insisted he needed, were similarly liberal about mixing drugs and weaponry. "With Phil," Cohen recalled years later, "especially in the state that he found himself, which was post-Wagnerian, I would say Hitlerian, the atmosphere was one of guns, I mean that's really what was going on, was guns. The music was subsidiary, an enterprise, you know people were armed to the teeth, all his friends, his bodyguards, and everybody was drunk, or intoxicated on other items, so you were slipping over bullets, and you were biting into revolvers in your hamburger. There were guns everywhere. Phil was beyond control. I remember the violin player in the song 'Fingerprints,' Phil didn't like the way he was playing, walked out into the studio, and pulled a gun on the guy. Now this was, he was a country boy, and he knew a lot about guns. He just put his fiddle in his case and walked out. That was the last we'd seen of him."[12]

Cohen himself was not exempt from feeling the barrel. One night, at around four in the morning, as another session cascaded to an end, Spector stumbled out of his booth and into the studio. In one hand, he held a .45 revolver, in the other, a half-empty bottle of Manischewitz sweet kosher wine. He put his arm around Cohen's shoulder and shoved the revolver into the singer's neck. "Leonard," he said, "I love you." Not missing a beat, Cohen replied, "I hope you do, Phil."[13]

But Spector's eccentricity in the studio wasn't the real problem. Each day, accompanied by his armed goons, he would take the master tapes to his car and whisk them away to his house. He had done the same thing with *Let It Be*. He would mix the album as he saw fit, and present it to Cohen as a fait accompli. It was not an arrangement any artist would gladly accept, especially when there were signs suggesting that somewhere amid the fog of booze and bullets, Spector lost track of any vision he might have had for the album. "I'll tell you something,

Larry," he wrote in a note he scribbled on the master tapes to his longtime engineer, Larry Levine. "We've done worse with better, and better with worse!"[14]

Cohen's fans, as well as some of the critics who reviewed the album upon its release, saw it as a farce. Here was Cohen's delicate poetry drowned by sound, his voice barely audible on some of the tracks. They were right, but for all the wrong reasons. Musically the album, *Death of a Ladies' Man*, is a marvel. "Memories," for example, is a grand doo-wop anthem, as well as a disquisition on pop history; it ends with a snippet from the Shields' 1958 hit "You Cheated, You Lied," which it closely resembles, and hearing the newer song melt into the older one delivers a brutal jolt of emotion. Here is doo-wop, two decades later, its promise all soured. It is sung now not by sweet-voiced youths but by a raspy-sounding middle-aged man. The melody, too, is louder and more frayed, almost hysterical. The Shields' song conveyed the genteel sadness of brokenhearted teenagers who grieved for an affair gone bad. They sensed, however unconsciously, that they had their entire lives ahead of them to fall in love all over again. Working with more or less the same tune, Cohen sounded desperate as he sang about walking up to the tallest and the blondest girl and asking to see her naked body. He cast himself as the same doo-wop crooner, twenty years older, realizing that heartbreak wasn't a sweet and passing sorrow but a permanent state of being, seeking now sex rather than romance.

This, then, was the real problem with *Death of a Ladies' Man*, not its musical styling but its spiritual message. Spector hadn't just made Cohen sound different; he made him sound crass. Cohen himself admitted as much: Playing "Memories" a few years later in Tel Aviv, he introduced the song with an apology. "Unfortunately," he said, "for my last song, I must offend your deepest sensibilities with an entirely irrelevant and vulgar ditty that I wrote some time ago with another Jew in Hollywood, where there are many. This is a song in which I have placed my most irrelevant and banal adolescent recollections. I humbly ask you for your indulgence. As I look back to the red acne of my adolescence, to the unmanageable desire of my early teens, to that time when every woman shone like the eternal light above the altar place and I myself was always on my knees before some altar, unimaginably more quiescent, potent, powerful and relevant than anything I could ever command."[15]

It was a real regression for an artist who had thought and written more intelligently about sex than most in the second half of the twentieth century. Carnal pleasures have always informed Cohen's work, even when they were conspicuously— and strangely—missing from the cultural landscape in which he moved. Sex, drugs, and rock and roll was only two parts true: For all the genre's lustful aura, it is hard to think of many rock songs that speak openly and candidly about copulation. It is hard to think of a Cohen song that does not: the sisters of mercy sweetening a fellow's night, Joplin giving head at the Chelsea, the lover moaning in midcoitus in *Death of a Ladies' Man*'s "Paper Thin Hotel." But the body is always only just a vessel for the soul; in "Paper Thin Hotel," for example, Cohen addresses his unfaithful lover by saying, "you are the naked woman in my heart / you are the angel with her legs apart."

Cohen's most eloquent statement on the connection between the spirit and the flesh, one of his most prominent and persistent preoccupations, was not musical but visual. For the cover of *New Skin for the Old Ceremony*, he had chosen an illustration taken from a sixteenth-century treatise on alchemy entitled *Rosarium Philosophorum*. One of ten drawings representing the cycle of life, the image Cohen had selected shows a naked man and woman in a sexual embrace. The text had great influence on Carl Gustav Jung, who used it as a basis for his theory of transference. The first stages, Jung wrote, in which the man and the woman stood separately, each in his or her own solitude, represented the "pluralistic state of the man who has not yet attained inner unity, hence the state of bondage and disunion, of disintegration, and of being torn in different directions—an agonizing, unredeemed state which longs for union, reconciliation, redemption, healing and wholeness."[16] Only when the man and the woman shed their clothes and become entwined does the healing start—theirs is a union of opposites that represents the relaxed chaos from which rebirth could now begin. "The unified male/female figure," as one scholar eloquently put it, "is a symbol of the union of the masculine consciousness with the feminine unconscious, indicating that just as the projected contents of the personal unconscious have to be integrated, so too must the projections emanating from the collective unconscious. The successful reclamation of these projected images gives birth to a new, enlarged psychic condition, which Jung calls the self. But rather than describing the self as a point midway between the conscious and the unconscious, here the self—as the term for the union of all opposites—reaches out beyond the individual to the world at large. It is not that the psyche has been displaced as the locus of ultimacy but that the self has taken on cosmic dimensions."[17] Put simply, copulation places each of its participants in a context larger then themselves, projects them onto the universe, frees them of their solipsistic shackles. Copulation is the gateway to redemption; when Spector reduced it to hard-ons and lechery, he bruised the part of Cohen's work that was most vital and tender. The *Rosarium* itself, after all, is famous for stating that *Aurum nostrum non est aurum vulgi*, "Our gold is not the gold of the vulgar."

Trying to recapture his sense of sanctity, Cohen published a book shortly after the Spector album. It was called *Death of a Lady's Man*, and consisted mainly of poetry juxtaposed with commentary and criticism, turning the collection into a little, self-contained Talmud. "I am almost 90," declares the book's final poem. "Everyone I know has died off / except Leonard / He can still be seen / hobbling with his love."[18]

And hobble on he did. Now the father of two children—his daughter, Lorca, named after his poetic idol, was born in 1974—he tried to reconcile with Suzanne but found the union too tense. Hers, he noted, were "Miami consumer habits. My only luxuries are airplane tickets to go anywhere at any time. All I need is a table, chair and bed."[19] In 1978, shortly after Cohen's mother, Masha, passed away, he and Suzanne separated. "I believed in him," she told an interviewer. "He had moved people in the right direction, toward gentleness. But then I became very alone—the proof of the poetry just wasn't there."[20] Nor, for very long, was Suzanne: Later that year she took her children, now aged seven and four, and moved to Avignon, France.

Crushed, Cohen folded himself into his suitcase. He wandered from Greece to New York to Los Angeles. He was forty-four years old, with a string of tepidly received albums to his name and, he confessed, "almost no personal life."[21] All he could do was write and arrange and record. The fruit of his efforts appeared the following year, in the fall of 1979; it was called *Recent Songs*.

If the album proved anything, it proved that Cohen had learned how to be sad in a fuller way. Songs like "I Came So Far for Beauty" and "Our Lady of Solitude" were paeans to failure, sung softly and without bitterness or malice. The kid who, decades earlier, thundered in the Jewish Library in Montreal and declared that loneliness was the only path to the divine was now a man who had lived long enough to realize that he had been right. Sex may take us beyond ourselves and make us of the world, but solitude made us of the heavens. It was not without its beauty, and not really opposed to living with others. It was merely a practice, a ritual human beings had to master before they could form more perfect unions.

The album's best expression of this elusive idea is a song that, on first hearing, sounds like a joke. The mariachi band that launches "Un Canadien Errant" does little to prepare listeners for Cohen's nasal French, and even less to explain why a lament about never again seeing Canada is delivered in the style of Mexico. But Cohen himself may have solved the riddle when he later said that Canada "has an experimental side to it. We are free from the blood myth, the soil myth, so we could start over somewhere else. We could purchase a set of uninhabited islands in the Caribbean. Or we could disperse throughout the cosmos and establish a mental Canada in which we communicate through fax machines."[22] It was more or less the same thing he had said in his 1964 speech about the prophets and the priests: You had to make your own loneliness if you had any hope of ever communicating again.

It's a difficult notion to comprehend, and yet it is one of the central tenets of Cohen's thought. Whatever else he may be he is also, perhaps first and foremost, the poet of loneliness. In his 1984 poetry collection, *Book of Mercy*, he wrote: "Blessed are you who has given each man a shield of loneliness so that he cannot forget you. You are the truth of loneliness, and only your name addresses it. Strengthen my loneliness that I may be healed in your name, which is beyond all consolations that are uttered on this earth. Only in your name can I stand in the rush of time, only when this loneliness is yours can I lift my sins toward your mercy."[23]

Others have mused about loneliness before, but seldom quite in this way. In recent decades we had Elliott Smith and the Smiths to listen to if we wanted to hear sensitive artists muse about the solitary life. But their worldview is modern, as it laments alienation and longs for connection. They seek whatever companionship they can find because they know, as the Smiths so eloquently put it, that when one is lonely, "life is very long."[24] Cohen's approach is more timeless and far more profound. Loneliness, he knows, is not a condition one can cure, but the essence of all being. It's the same position argued by John Milton: As God and Adam converse at one point in *Paradise Lost*, the first man complains that all of the newly created world's wonders are charmless when enjoyed alone. The Almighty, "not displeased," makes a short speech, a wonder in a book dense with wonders:

A nice and subtle happiness I see
Thou to thyself proposest, in the choice
Of thy Associates, Adam, and wilt taste
No pleasure, though in pleasure, solitary.
What think'st thou then of mee, and this my State,
Seem I to thee sufficiently possesed
Of happiness, or not? who am alone
From all Eternitie, for none I know
Second to me or like, equal much less.
How have I then with whom to hold converse
Save with the Creatures which I made, and those
To me inferior, infinite descents
Beneath what other Creatures are to thee?[25]

God, then, is the loneliest of us all. His loneliness is essential: By definition there is no one like him, no one who can understand his language, no one who can even see his face. And yet he creates, forging a universe packed with beings he knows to be far inferior to himself. For much of Christian theology, this is the source of grace—God the ever-loving awards the gift of life to us sinful and wretched creatures, forever undeserving of his kindness. For Judaism, however, this is a call to action: Like God, the pious must learn to be in loneliness while striving all the while to create the world around them. It's a tough undertaking for anyone, but particularly so for artists, whose daily routine involves the forging of new worlds parallel to their own. To cope, Cohen needed a program, a method of shedding light on the world when inside him all was silent and dark. He found it in Rinzai Buddhism.

Cohen's involvement with the Japanese sect began in the

late 1960s, when a mutual friend introduced him to Kyozan Joshu Sasaki, known as Roshi, or "venerable teacher." Born on a farm in northern Japan in 1907, Roshi followed the events of World War I with great interest and dreamed of becoming a solider. He idolized Germany, which he imagined to be a mighty nation rendered omnipotent by its warplanes and guns. As the war progressed and descended into senseless bloodshed, and as his brother became ill and died, Roshi changed his mind and decided to apprentice himself to a local Buddhist abbot. As part of his initiation, he was presented with a question: How old is the Buddha? "His ready answer stunned his master and put him on the path to early priesthood," a newspaper report later described it. "'Buddha's age and my age,'" replied the young boy, "'are the same.'"[26] The answer revealed not only an innate wisdom—perceiving of age not as a chronological order but as a state of constant flux in which one is always, like the Buddha, ready to learn and evolve—but also a compatibility with Rinzai's particular style of teaching. There are numerous subtle differences between Rinzai and the other school of Zen Buddhism, Soto, mainly concerning the manner of practice. While Soto spoke softly, Rinzai shouted, with its earliest teachers often insulting or assaulting students. Soto sought harmony in sitting *zazen* and contemplating quietly, while Rinzai put more weight on the *koan*. Just what was the sound of one hand clapping? If you understood this wasn't a riddle to be solved but a meditation designed to carry you past the strictures of rationality and into real insight, you were on the path to awakening.

And Cohen understood. He had never abandoned Judaism— this was frequently suggested when his involvement with

Roshi became known, and it irked him every time. "My father and mother, of blessed memory," he wrote in a letter to the *Hollywood Reporter* in 1993, "would have been disturbed by the Reporter's description of me as a Buddhist. I am a Jew. For some time now I have been intrigued by the indecipherable ramblings of an old zen monk. Not long ago he said to me, 'Cohen, I have known you for 23 years and I never tried to give you my religion. I just poured you sake.' Saying that, he filled my cup with sake. I bowed my head and raised my cup to him crying out, 'Rabbi, you are surely the Light of the Generation.'"[27] He wasn't being facetious: The lyricist who habitually wrote dozens of verses for each song before eliminating all but the best couldn't have asked for a better teacher. "Roshi's great," Cohen said on another occasion. "If you have an appetite for that kind of simplification in your life, to hang out with a guy who doesn't really speak good English, whom you like very much, is a good way to discipline your speech or writing. You've got to get very, very clear if you hang out and drink with somebody who doesn't really speak English. So the conversation gets very intuitive and very clear. And to be able to write that way is a great goal."[28]

There was more, however, to his affiliation with Roshi than the satisfaction that came with a life dedicated to the pursuit of clarity. Far from incompatible with Judaism, the old master's views underscored many of the central mysteries with which Cohen had struggled since being steeped in the old religion as a child, including the question concerning the nature of God. "The moment someone says the truth or God is an object or takes it as an object, that is already a mistake," Roshi told a newspaper reporter visiting him a few months after his one-hundredth birthday. "God is neither object nor subject. The moment you say any little thing about God, you're already making an object of God and Buddhism cautions you about that. At that moment you're making an idiot out of God, you're making a fool out of God."[29] To think like that is to understand that Judaism's essential questions—why were the chosen people chosen, to what end, and for how long— were themselves, to some extent, *koans*. No Jew was expected to interpret the precise nature of divine election just as no Buddhist was expected to decipher the sound of one hand clapping; it was something to ponder, a drawbridge past the moats of reason and into some realm of higher understanding, impossible to describe in words. It's that realm that so much of Leonard Cohen's music seeks to explore, not just for Jews but for humankind, and not in the priestly way, by reciting the ancient texts, but prophetically, by following an ever-moving God wherever he went. This is what Cohen's Jesus is getting at, perhaps, when he declares, in "Suzanne," that "all men will be sailors then / Until the sea shall free them." It is also why he sinks beneath our wisdom like a stone: Redemption never was and will never be a business for critical thinkers. "As long as we see things dualistically," read a line in the official journal of Roshi's monastery on Mount Baldy, "we shall never see the truth. . . . In the state of zero, there are no questions."[30] But how to get to a state of zero? For Leonard Cohen, that was what the next two decades were about.

CHAPTER NINE

"A Secret Chord"

John Lissauer realized that Leonard Cohen was a changed man as soon as he saw the Casio. It was 1984, and he was intrigued to hear from the singer after almost a decade without word. Lissauer knew about Cohen's turbulent personal life, and expected to meet a more weathered man, but nothing prepared him for the sight of the troubadour exchanging his guitar for one of those toy gizmos that were hawked in tourist-trap shops all along Broadway and that sounded tinny and flat. Cohen, Lissauer recalled, pressed a button, and the machine spat out a tacky rhythm. Then Cohen played a new song. It was called "Dance Me to the End of Love," and it sounded very different from Cohen's earlier work.

It wasn't only the change of instrument. There was something more mature about the song. Despite the "me" in the title, it was a different Leonard doing the singing, one who seemed at once more present and almost entirely abstract. Cohen alluded to this transformation in "I Bury My Girlfriend," one of the poems in *Death of a Lady's Man*: "You ask me how I write. This is how I write. I get rid of the lizard. I eschew the philosopher's stone. I bury my girlfriend. I remove my personality from the line so that I am permitted to use the first person as often as I wish without offending my appetite for modesty. Then I resign. I do errands for my mother, or someone like her. I eat too much. I blame those closest to me for ruining my talent. Then you come to me. The joyous news is mine."

Using the first person, Cohen knew, offended more than just his modesty. It was wounding his sense of purpose as an artist. Again and again he reflected on the oddity of having to share intimate sentiments with arenas packed thick with strangers, singing "Suzanne" and "So Long, Marianne"—one woman his friend and the other his lover, both songs written with their specific muses in mind—repeatedly as throngs of people who had met neither woman shouted the words back at him from their seats.

This crisis of intimacy affected other rock stars as well. Some, like Bowie or the Beatles, solved it temporarily by pretending to be other people. "We were fed up with being the Beatles," Paul McCartney said when asked about the origins of Sgt. Pepper and the Lonely Hearts Club Band. "We really hated that fucking four little Mop-Top boys approach. We were not boys, we were men. It was all gone, all that boy shit, all that screaming, we didn't want any more, plus, we'd now got turned on to pot and thought of ourselves as artists rather than just performers. There was now more to it; not only had John and I been writing, George had been writing, we'd been in films, John had written books, so it was natural that we should become artists. Then suddenly on the plane I got this idea. I thought, Let's not be ourselves. Let's develop alter egos so we're not having to project an image which we know. It would be much more free."[1] Fewer still took Dylan's approach and came to see songs as consumer goods that could be tweaked at will, rebranded and resold whenever the changing tastes of the market so decreed or the whims of the artist so dictated. When Larry "Ratso" Sloman, for example, learned that Dylan had decided to cut the masterpiece "Blind Willie McTell" from *Infidels*, he confronted the artist and asked him for a reason. "It's just an album," Dylan said. "I've made thirty of them."[2]

But Cohen couldn't play fast and loose with his work, and he couldn't play dress-up. He had to find some other way to sing without frequently feeling as if he were betraying his material, his audience, or both. The new songs he played for Lissauer in 1984 suggested that he had. If the guitar had been the instrument with which to write songs that played out like diary entries, the Casio was a portal to a higher plane of consciousness. Cohen's new songs, Dylan noted when he heard them, sounded like prayers. Some more than others: "If It Be Your Will," for example, perfectly mimicked the cadences and preoccupations of Jewish prayers. "If it be your will," Cohen sang, "If there is a choice / Let the rivers fill / Let the hills rejoice / Let your mercy spill / On all these burning hearts in hell / If it be your will / To make us well."

Cohen had experimented with this mode of writing before. He had described "Bird on the Wire" as being "simultaneously a prayer and an anthem," and had written several other songs that courted the liturgical. But something always got in the way. No matter where the earlier songs started out, they ended up being confessions, delivered gracefully by the sinner himself, accompanied by strings. The new songs were unencumbered; they did not feel obliged to tell a story or create a mood or do anything but deliver their wisdom. Like real prayers, once written they seemed no longer to belong to their composer but instead to become the property of whoever cared to softly mouth their words. Cohen realized that well; when *Q* magazine asked him, in 1994, what song he wished he had written, Cohen replied, "'If It Be Your Will.' And I wrote it."[3]

This new mode of writing echoed not only ancient traditions but distinctly contemporary ones as well, corresponding with the dictates of modernist poetry. "One error, in fact, of eccentricity in poetry is to seek for new human emotions to express," T. S. Eliot famously wrote in 1921, "and in this search for novelty in the wrong place it discovers the perverse. The business of the poet is not to find new emotions, but to use the ordinary ones and, in working them up into poetry, to express feelings which are not in actual emotions at all. And emotions which he has never experienced will serve his turn as well as those familiar to him. . . . There is a great deal, in the writing of poetry, which must be conscious and deliberate. In fact, the bad poet is usually unconscious where he ought to be conscious, and conscious where he ought to be unconscious. Both errors tend to make him 'personal.' Poetry is not a turning loose of emotion, but an escape from emotion; it is not the expression of personality, but an escape from personality. But, of course, only those who have personality and emotions know what it means to want to escape from these things."[4] Anyone who wished to remain a poet after the age of twenty-five, Eliot quipped in the same essay, had to realize that the past was always present; he might have added that anyone who wished to remain a rock star after the age of forty-five had to make a similar concession.

Cohen did. For the first time in his work, the past and the

present merged. "Bird on the Wire," for example, owes much of its power to the stark contrast between the things Cohen confessed to having done—"I have torn everyone who reached out for me"—and the promises he was now making—"But I swear by this song / And by all that I have done wrong / I will make it all up to thee." And "The Sisters of Mercy" thrills because of its temporal tension between the singer's recollection of his first and mystical encounter with the women in the song's title and his admonitions to us who are about to meet them. But "Hallelujah," one of the new songs Cohen had played for Lissauer, follows a different logic. "I heard there was a secret chord," Cohen begins, "that David played and it pleased the Lord / But you don't really care for music, do you?" The transcendent and the earthly intermingling was Cohen's oldest trick—he'd used it everywhere from his earliest poetry to "Suzanne," which is both about a friend and her habits and about Christ and his anguish—but he cuts it short. The very next verse does something strange. "Your faith was strong but you needed proof," it begins, "You saw her bathing on the roof." From merely singing about the biblical king, Cohen continues by addressing him directly—the bather on the roof, we assume, is Bathsheba—condemning us to spend the rest of the song steeped in confusion. Who is he talking to or about? Himself? Some unnamed lover? King David? Another biblical figure—a later reference to the cutting of hair implies Samson? We never know. He could be talking to anyone, and the song could be taking place anytime and anywhere.

"I always said, everyone's going to find a way to do this song," Lissauer recalled. "The way we tailored the sound was very bizarre. I just wanted Leonard to be the voice. Not necessarily the voice of God, but it's the voice, and it really does take you places. And we avoided doing the gospel choir thing. It was just a choir of regular people. There were some kids, a couple of friends, and the guys in the band. At one point we did toy with the idea of having a glorious choir, but I said no, let's make it everyman. So that it wasn't bigger than life. So that it was everyone's hallelujah."[5]

Judging by the obscene number of cover versions, the song is everyone's indeed. But it only takes a passing acquaintance with the other "Hallelujahs" to realize just how towering Cohen's achievement truly was. A favorite with contestants of televised singing competitions, the song tends to inspire the sort of cascade of crescendos that causes inexperienced and dramatic singers to shut their eyes tightly and clench their fists as they belt out verse after verse. Overcome with emotion, they take the song—as had its best-known interpreter, Jeff Buckley—to be about the hallelujah of the orgasm, the turning loose of emotion T. S. Eliot so rightly disdained. Cohen himself has none of that. He sings it simply and straightforwardly, so that the last verse is strongest: "I did my best, it wasn't much / I couldn't feel, so I tried to touch / I've told the truth, I didn't come to fool you / And even though it all went wrong / I'll stand before the Lord of Song / With nothing on my tongue but Hallelujah."

It's a startling end to such a song; we expect a measure of resolution, or at least a concluding statement about love. Instead Cohen ends up all by himself, talking to God, admitting defeat. He couldn't feel, so he wrote a song, understanding that the Holy Ghost may preside over the occasional copulation, but that if humans were ever to meet their maker—the Lord of Song—the way to do it was through ritual, imperfect and frequently devoid of emotion but ultimately and cosmically effective. When an interviewer told Cohen, years later, that "Hallelujah" conveyed a sense of holiness, it was ritual that Cohen wanted to talk about instead. "I understand that they forgot how to build the arch for several hundred years," he said. "Masons forgot how to do certain kinds of arches, it was lost. So it is in our time that certain spiritual mechanisms that were very useful have been abandoned and forgot. Redemption, repentance, resurrection. All those ideas are thrown out with the bathwater. People became suspicious of religion plus all these redemptive mechanisms that are very useful."[6]

Cohen was now committed to the mechanisms. When he took the album on tour, he decided to perform in Poland, becoming one of very few Western artists to visit the Communist nation. Lech Wałesa, the leader of Solidarity, asked to appear onstage with Cohen, but the singer refused. His Polish fans and critics alike argued, with varying degrees of generosity, that he realized an overt political statement would anger the authorities and likely lead to the cancellation of his shows. He did not seem concerned about the authorities, though. Speaking to the massive audience in Warsaw's palatial Sala Kongresowa on March 22, 1985, Cohen said:

I come from a country where we do not have the same struggles as you have. I respect your struggles. And it may surprise you, but I respect both sides of this struggle. It seems to me that in Europe there needs to be a left foot and a right foot to move forward. I wish that both feet moved forward and the body moved towards its proper destiny. This is an intense country; the people are heroic, the spirit is independent. It is a difficult country to govern. It needs a strong government and a strong union. When I was a child I went to synagogue every Saturday morning. Once in this country, there were thousands of synagogues, and thousands of Jewish communities which were wiped out in a few months. In the synagogue which I attended there was a prayer for the government. We were happy and we are happy to pray for the welfare of the government. And I would like to say to you, to the leaders of the left, and the leaders of the right, I sing for everyone. My song has no flag, my song has no party. And I say the prayer that we said in our synagogue, I say it for the leader of your union and the leader of your party. May the Lord put a spirit of wisdom and understanding into the hearts of your leaders and into the hearts of all their counselors.[7]

He sang a few more songs and took pleasure in light banter—at one point jokingly thanking the Russians for building such a glamorous stadium for his exclusive use—but he did not wish to let go of his introductory theme:

You know, since I've been here many people have asked me what I thought just about everything there is in this vale of tears. I don't know the answers to anything. I've just come here to sing you these songs that have been inspired by something that I hope is deeper and bigger than myself. I have nothing to say about the way that Poland is governed. I have nothing to say about the resistance to the government. The relationship between the people and its government is an intimate thing. It is not for a stranger to comment. I know there is an eye that watches all of us. There is a judgment that weighs everything we do. And before this great force, which is greater than any government, I stand in awe and I kneel in respect and it is to this great judgment that I dedicate the next song.[8]

The next song was "Hallelujah."

As Cohen completed his tour and returned stateside, the eye that watches all of us seemed to be watching him more closely. His former backup singer, Jennifer Warnes, released *Famous Blue Raincoat*, an album of Cohen covers, in January 1987. It was a hit: Warnes's sweet, earthy American voice was just the coating many listeners needed to swallow Cohen's complex lyrics. Delivered by the man himself, the song that gave the album its title, for example, is a cool and haunted piece. Even if you didn't know that the line about going clear was a reference to Scientology—a pursuit Cohen had briefly explored—you could still feel its weight, still intuit that Cohen had something in mind that far transcended a report on a relationship. There was a dynamic of enlightenment in his song. You listened to it with a detached distance, waiting for a big reveal that would explain what it was all about, only to be stung by that final line, "Sincerely, L. Cohen," that announced that the sermon was over and your only shot at comprehension was to listen to it again. Jennifer Warnes's version, however, requires no second listening. It is immediately comprehensible. It replaces Cohen's spiritual intricacies with an emphasis, just as potent and no less sublime, on emotional urgency. To hear Warnes sing it, "Famous Blue Raincoat" is the sort of melancholic reflection one has not too long after a painful breakup, when the details are still hazy and the feelings are still raw. Hers was a very different song, and a significantly more popular one.

By all accounts Cohen was thrilled with Warnes's success, and contributed an illustration to the album's liner notes, a doodle of one hand passing a torch on to another with the caption "Jenny sings Lenny." The album also contained a previously unreleased Cohen composition, titled "First We Take Manhattan" and conceived together with a few other songs that were beginning to give a new Cohen album its shape. But Cohen himself was teetering on the verge of darkness, his lifelong struggle with depression entering one of its most jagged stretches. "I couldn't get out of bed and couldn't leave the house," Cohen told an interviewer years later. "And that was the best part of it. The drug that [the doctor] gave me seemed to put a bottom on how low I could go and a ceiling on how high I could go. I felt like I was living in an aquarium full of cotton wool. I seemed to be able to get a little bit of work done, not too much. At a certain moment one night, I just threw away the safety net of the pills. And then I came around. I don't want to emphasize this but the work does tend to break you down. Maybe the work is a bit about breaking down. Somehow when you have broken down, you find a place where you can't lie. Otherwise your defenses are so skillful and your bullshit is so abundant that you can come up with something."[9]

The album that emerged was bereft of bullshit. There was a new inflection in his voice that wasn't there before, an Old Testament type of growl. When he delivered lines like "You loved me as a loser, but now you're worried that I just might win / You know the way to stop me, but you don't have the discipline," or "Now you can say that I've grown bitter but of this you may be sure / The rich have got their channels in the bedrooms of the poor / And there's a mighty judgment coming, but I may be wrong," Cohen was acknowledging not only that he had some knowledge worth listening to, but that there were mighty forces at play, the forces of a decadent culture, committed to curbing his speech. Finally Cohen had slipped into his Isaiah mode.

Like the prophets of the Old Testament, and unlike Christ, Cohen, in his new designation as parser of eternal truths, warmed up to the realization that any expectation of rapturous redemption was misguided. Having danced around the question of salvation in many of his early songs—all that business about us forgetting to pray for the angels and the angels forgetting to pray for us—Cohen finally found his meaning in the ancient words of the Gemara, a compendium of rabbinical commentaries compiled between 200 and 600 CE, which, addressing the possibility of the messiah, remarked, "Let him come, but let me not see him in my lifetime." Redemption, the rabbis understood, was terrifying, a vast unknown lying far beyond human comprehension. There was no point in mortals pondering the end-times. All that humans could do was go about life, admit defeat, and try to find beauty in all that remained.

This spirit was reminiscent of Cohen's Zen awakening; a favorite response to the question of what is Zen held that it was no more than vast emptiness and nothing special. And it was in this spirit that the songs of Cohen's new album, *I'm*

Your Man, released in February 1988, presented themselves. "Take This Waltz," Cohen's translation of a Lorca poem, urged listeners to seize the dance, as "it's yours now, it's all that there is." The lyric is not an invitation to give up hope. As Cohen's translation of Lorca's gorgeous poem so clearly demonstrates, one can marvel at the beauty of the world even while admitting that the world is irreparably broken. "You really don't command the enterprise," Cohen said in an interview decades later. "Sometimes, when you no longer see yourself as the hero of your own drama, you know, expecting victory after victory, and you understand deeply that this is not paradise, somehow, especially the privileged ones that we are, we somehow embrace the notion that this vale of tears is perfectible, that you're going to get it all straight. I found that things became a lot easier when I no longer expected to win."[10]

Profoundly un-American as that last sentence may be, it resonated strongly with members of the new generation that came to the cultural fore as the 1980s gave way to the 1990s. Their parents, the former hippies and marchers and shouters and dabblers and optimists of the 1960s, had been, perhaps, the last uncomplicatedly American generation. Even as they protested against their country's policies or burned its flags, they were exuding the same exuberant spirit that had, throughout the centuries, propelled it to such great heights. They were easily recognizable in Walt Whitman's celebration of Americans as those young men and women who were perpetually "stuffed with the stuff that is coarse, and stuffed with the stuff that is fine, / One of the great nation, the nation of many nations— / the smallest the same and the largest the same."[11] But as Greil Marcus observed in his book about the Doors, the sixties had left in its aftermath "this almost physical sense of an absence . . . a silence that ultimately silences all the endlessly programmed Sixties hits, that mocks their flash."[12] Prog rock, punk, and everything else that followed in the two decades since the Doors played their last concert in 1970 were the final spasms of a dying body. By the time the children of the flower children were old enough to look for meaning in music, all they could hear was silence.

This, more or less, is the premise of the 1990 cult film *Pump Up the Volume*. Its protagonist, Mark Hunter, is an awkward high school student in a suburb of Phoenix, played with perfect pubescent angst by Christian Slater. At night, however, the shy guy blooms to life as he operates a pirate radio station out of his bedroom, calling himself Happy Harry Hard-On and ranting about the pointlessness of it all. "Did you ever get the feeling that everything in America is completely fucked up?" asks one typical oration. "You know that feeling that the whole country is like one inch away from saying 'That's it, forget it.' You think about it. Everything is polluted. The environment, the government, the schools, you name it."[13] Happy Harry's only path to salvation, the only way of escaping from the rubble of shattered promises left behind by his parents and their generation, is to listen to music that is good and true and that knows something about the world. The film's sound track, the alt-rock Rosetta stone of the 1990s, featured a wide gallery of young musicians with unimpeachable indie credentials—Cowboy Junkies, Henry Rollins, Peter Murphy. But when Happy Harry had to choose a theme song for his broadcast, he turned to Cohen's "Everybody Knows."

It was a perfectly placed bit of cultural shorthand. By 1990

Cohen had become the slim, aging guru to a generation of artists working to redefine what they considered to be a musical
scene corrupted by too much money, too little integrity, and
no good ideas. They were supported by a fan base culled from
the best-educated generation of Americans in history—college
attendance rates, hovering at 45.1 percent in 1959, shot past
the 60 percent mark by the late 1980s—and relied on a net-
work of campus radio stations to carry their music directly to
its target audience.

And they believed neither in the excesses of glam and prog
rock nor in the ideological and aesthetic deprivations of punk.
Instead, like so many artists working in postmodernism's
shadow, they were obsessed with the notion of authenticity,
and believed that their music's chief yardstick was its ability to
convey emotions without compromise. When these artists—an
imperfect chronology would probably begin with R.E.M. and
end with Nirvana—looked backward for inspiration, they found
few forefathers more worthy than Cohen.

One of these fans—a young Dubliner who had tired of the
endless guitar solos that seemed to encumber every song in the
early 1970s, started his own high school band to play covers of
the Beach Boys and the Rolling Stones, and then began playing
original music, changing the band's name from the Hype to
U2 and his own from Paul David Hewson to Bono—captured
Cohen's appeal eloquently. "He has you at any stage in your
life," Bono said in a 2005 interview. "He has your youthful
idealism. He has you when your relationship is splitting up, he
has you when you can't face the world and you're looking for
something higher to get through. He has you at all stages."[14]
For a boy like Bono, who was fourteen when he lost his mother

to an aneurysm, and belonged to a street gang of intellectual, surrealist-minded friends, the past was thick with madmen and fakers. The former, men like Jim Morrison, were more cautionary tales than role models; the latter merited no further thought. But Cohen seemed to offer a worldview that was as interested in what went on above as it did in what happened below: "Real spirituality," Cohen once told an interviewer, "has its feet in the mud and its heart in heaven."[15] It was a very Irish sensibility, but also one that embodied the new style of music, lean and truthful, that clever and disillusioned young men and women wanted to make in the 1980s and early 1990s.

Years later, and perhaps the world's biggest rock star, Bono would cover "Hallelujah" in concert, often using it, shrewdly and elegantly, as an invocation of sorts and singing a bar or two before proceeding into one of his own compositions.[16] Cohen's song, he said, was "so surprising because as well as bringing you to your knees, [Cohen] makes you laugh. And that's the shock. You see, lots of people, lots of writers, have dared to walk up to the edge of reason and stare into that great chasm, into the abyss. Very few people have got there and laughed out loud at what they saw. It's the divine comedy." It's hard not to think of James Joyce, whom both Cohen and Bono revere,[17] sitting in his study, staring past the edge of reason as he was writing *Finnegans Wake*, and laughing heartily through the night, night after night.

Like Joyce, Cohen's career was met first by befuddlement and scorn and only later—in both cases thanks to the intervention of contemporary tastemakers—by universal admiration. Looking at him in the early 1990s, Cohen seemed very much a man in full. Inducted into the Canadian Music Hall of Fame in

1991, he no longer seemed conflicted, as he had been decades before, about being the recipient of his nation's most rarified honors, and accepted his laurels with a smile. "If I had been given this attention when I was 26," he said, "it would have turned my head. At 36 it might have confirmed my flight on a rather morbid spiritual path. At 46 it would have rubbed my nose in my failing powers and have prompted a plotting of a getaway and an alibi. But at 56—hell, I'm just hitting my stride and it doesn't hurt at all."[18]

The following year he accompanied his new girlfriend, the actress Rebecca De Mornay, to the Academy Awards ceremony; the tabloids were delighted with the odd pairing, happy to assign Cohen to the same coterie of aging rock stars who were cashing in on their cool by dating young and ravishing women. Cohen and De Mornay had even become engaged, a first for Cohen despite a life rich with long, committed relationships. He seemed ready to plunge into matrimony, into committed couplehood. He seemed, as a *Los Angeles Times* headline put it, "pain free."[19]

He was not. His particular surge of renown had defined him out of existence, turning him into a largely meaningless icon, an easy target for accolades. By the time he got around to shooting a music video for "Closing Time," he was so famous that even his own crew had no idea who he was. The song was a country-and-western tune, all about whiskey and dancing and the devil, and the shoot was booked at a Toronto club called the Matador. It was winter, and dozens of men and women—extras, assistants, musicians, hangers-on—were packed on the club's floor, hemmed in by two large Greek-style columns. To keep the place in order, the production had set up two tables, one at each end of the room. One was marked "Crew Only" and was loaded with nuts, vegetables, dips, and other goods; the other, marked "Extras Only," offered more humble refreshments like chips and Cheesies. Dressed in a dark-gray striped double-breasted suit and a black T-shirt, Cohen moseyed over to the crew's table, selected a celery stick, and took a bite.

Immediately a production assistant pounced. "Excuse me," the man demanded officiously. "Are you an extra?"

"Yeah," Cohen said. "I'm an extra."

"Well," said the production assistant, "would you *please* get your food from the extras' tray."[20]

Cohen obeyed. And he wasn't being coy—or not only. He truly felt superfluous: Now in his midfifties, he'd reached that most uncanny of plateaus for rock stars—no longer a vibrant youth, not yet a dignified elder. His songs, too, were in limbo: Interviewed about his craft, he admitted that his work, always a painstaking and prolonged process, now trickled even slower. New songs took him a decade to write. "Closing Time," for example, had begun life as "a perfectly reasonable song. And a good one, I might say. A respectable song. But I choked over it. There wasn't anything that really addressed my attention. The finishing of it was agreeable because it's always an agreeable feeling. But when I tried to sing it I realized it came from my boredom and not from my attention. It came from my desire to finish the song and not from the *urgency* to locate a construction that would engross me. So I went to work again."[21] That lack of urgency was more than mere artistic malaise: It was existential.

"I used to be able to write songs on the run," he said, not letting on that the opposite was true and that each song took him a short eternity to complete. "I used to work hard but I didn't really begin slaving over them till 1983. I always used to work hard. But I had no idea what hard work was until something changed in my mind." That something, he continued, was a sense "that this whole enterprise is limited, that there was an end in sight. . . . That you were really truly mortal. I don't know what it was exactly, I'm just speculating. But at a certain moment I found myself engaged in songwriting in the same way that I had been engaged in novel writing when I was very young. In other words, it's something you do every day and you can't get too far from it, otherwise you forget *what it's about*."[22]

Even as Cohen was thinking about life's end and the hard, constant work he was engaged in, his fandom among fellow musicians continued to swell. A 1991 tribute album, *I'm Your Fan*, featured Cohen covers by the Pixies, Nick Cave, R.E.M., and James. It was well reviewed. By 1995 Cohen's allure as a musicians' musician was so luminous that a second tribute album, *Tower of Song*, attracted Billy Joel, Elton John, and Sting. It was a hellish match. The album, wrote one critic, capturing the consensus, was "a total train wreck," showcasing "big-name engines" that "barrel down the track, horns blaring, with no regard for such warning signals as color, shade, contrast, tone, definition. A complete derailment, because what they've all missed is the poetry of Cohen's lyrics."[23]

In 1992 Cohen released *The Future*. A decade of rewrites had paid off: The songs were sharp and unafraid of loudly declaring their preoccupations. "You don't know me from the wind," declares the track that lends the album its name, "You never will, you never did / I'm the little Jew who wrote the Bible / I've seen the nations rise and fall / I've heard their stories, heard them all / But love's the only engine of survival." Another song, "Anthem," was even more bluntly prophetic: "Ring the bells that still can ring," it declared, "Forget your perfect offering / There is a crack in everything / That's how the light gets in." Cohen was channeling millennia of Jewish thought—the crack is a favorite kabbalistic metaphor—and composing an anthem that celebrated what most anthems dared not acknowledge, namely the irreparable condition of human life. "The light," he told an interviewer, "is the capacity to reconcile your experience, your sorrow, with every day that dawns. It is that understanding, which is beyond significance or meaning, that allows you to live a life and embrace the disasters and sorrows and joys that are our common lot. But it's only with the recognition that there is a crack in everything. I think all other visions are doomed to irretrievable gloom."[24]

It was a vision too subtle for many of his fans to embrace. In 1994, two decades after Robert Altman artfully used Cohen's songs in *McCabe & Mrs. Miller*, and four years after Allan Moyle harnessed them to *Pump Up the Volume*, Oliver Stone tethered Cohen's music to his new film, *Natural Born Killers*. As one fan, Ted Ekering, had noted,[25] Stone shared with Cohen a dismay with art's inability to capture the most fundamental of human emotions. Just as Cohen had done with *Flowers for Hitler*, Stone designed *Natural Born Killers* as antiart, making sure that each cut called attention to itself and stacking the film with references to other films, including his own. "I been thinking 'bout why they're makin' all these stupid fuckin' movies," muses the movie's lead character, Mickey, played by Woody Harrelson, as he watches Brian De Palma's *Scarface* in his hotel room. "Doesn't anybody out there in Hollywood believe in kissin' anymore?" Stone himself, of course, had written that *Scarface*'s screenplay; the monologue, Ekering observed, wasn't that different from Cohen's gambit when he began one of his poems by stating that he had no more talent left. But Cohen had outgrown his despair, crept out of his experiments with form, and taught himself to write about human life with gentleness and persistence. Stone had neither the patience nor the capacity for such intricacies. In one particularly dismal scene, Cohen's "Waiting for the Miracle" plays as the two protagonists, both psychopathic serial killers, make love. "I know you really loved me," Cohen croons as they grind into each other; then, the camera pans, revealing a young woman, their victim, bound and gagged in the corner, terrified. Cohen's song continues: "But you see, my hands were tied." The same thing that had happened to "Hallelujah" was beginning to happen to Cohen's other songs, and to Cohen himself—he was being taken literally.

It was the worst thing that could happen to Cohen. With the reinvigorated interest in his music came a demand to see him live. In 1988, promoting *I'm Your Man*, he went on a twenty-five-date tour, with a leisurely four-month break in between; in 1993, supporting *The Future*, he played twenty-six shows in Europe, and then proceeded almost directly on an intensive two-month, thrity-seven-show tour of North America.[26] It was exhausting. Cohen drank. For reasons known only to them, he and De Mornay ended their engagement.

When he returned home, Cohen drove up to Mount Baldy, convinced that caring for Roshi was the panacea he needed. He stayed there for five years. He wore gray robes and marched with the other monks in a line amid the compound's gray rocks and slim trees. He sat at a long wooden table and drank water from a small bowl. He was silent most of the day, as were those around him. An artist trained in abandoning his art, Cohen might have decided to condemn his music to the same fate as his poetry and his novels. He could have stopped writing songs, or written rarely, or concluded that he no longer felt any need to communicate his enlightenment to others. But writing, he now realized, was ritual, remarkable less for bringing its practitioner closer to God than for enforcing a sort of maniacal discipline, a commitment to control and austerity not so different from the one constantly on display on Mount Baldy. Speaking to a reporter visiting him at his quarters there in 1996, he equated writing with sitting *zazen* and meditating. "You have to dive into it," he said. "You have to sit in the very bonfire of that distress, and you sit there until you're burnt away, and it's ashes, and it's gone."[27] By "it" he meant his songs: They, he stated repeatedly, were like ashes, blowing in the wind, blowing right through their listeners, pure in their essence but nothing more than remnants of a life once lived.

If the songs were ashes, Roshi, increasingly, was the fire. "I don't feel like acting on a sense of despair," Cohen said. "Or maybe this whole activity is a response to a sense of despair that I've always had. The quality of the relationship that is possible with Roshi is very instructive. He's both a friend and the enemy. He is just what he is. And of course he's going to be an enemy to your self-indulgence, an enemy to your laziness, he's going to be a friend to your effort. . . . He's going to be all the things that he has to be to turn you away from depending on him. And finally you just say this guy is absolutely true, he really loves me so much that I don't need to depend on him. His love is a liberating kind of love and his company is a liberating kind of company, so he's only interested in you making an effort to be yourself. So that's a very, very helpful kind of friend. And that's the kind of friend we should be to each other."[28]

The most important liberation his friend facilitated was the liberation from being Leonard Cohen. "As he said to me in one of our first personal encounters, formal encounters," Cohen recalled, "he said, 'I not Japanese, you not Jewish.' So, Roshi not Zen master, and Leonard not Zen student. Other versions of ourselves might arise that are more interesting. And so he became a part of my life and a deep friend in the real sense of friendship, someone who really cared, or didn't care, I am not quite sure which it is, who deeply didn't care about who I was, therefore who I was began to wither, and the less I was of who I was, the better I felt."[29] And on Mount Baldy, with Roshi, Cohen felt good, good enough to spend a significant portion of the 1990s there. For a decade, he neither performed nor released albums, but his old songs continued to win new fans. He had fulfilled the conditions of artistic ascendance described by Stephen Dedalus, Joyce's alter ego, in *A Portrait of the Artist as a Young Man*. "The personality of the artist," Dedalus opined, "at first a cry or a cadence or a mood and then a fluid and lambent narrative, finally refines itself out of existence, impersonalises itself, so to speak. The esthetic image in the dramatic form is life purified in and reprojected from the human imagination. The mystery of esthetic like that of material creation is accomplished. The artist, like the God of the creation, remains within or behind or beyond or above his handiwork, invisible, refined out of existence, indifferent, paring his fingernails."[30]

"Refined out of existence": That is what it must have felt like for Cohen on Mount Baldy. "It's a place where it's very difficult to hold fast to one's ideas," he said of his new home. "There is this sort of charitable void that I found here in a very pure form."[31] When a Swedish television journalist came to visit him, he mused that he might never again return to songwriting; he might, he said, get a real job, maybe at a bookstore. Or maybe he'd remain committed to his monastic undertakings: "I can't interrupt these studies," he said. "It's too important for me to interrupt. . . . For the health of my soul."[32]

But Cohen was never one for mere transcendence or for selves overcome. He was too much of a connoisseur of the flesh and of worldly joys. Even on the mountain, reflecting on emptiness, he was aware of, and amused by, his earthly affiliations. A poem he wrote, "Early Morning at Mt. Baldy," captures this sensibility well. After describing the elaborate ceremony of putting on his kimono and other ceremonial garb—the "serpentine belt," he observed, resembled a braided challah—he tumbles right down to the punch line: "all in all / about 20 pounds of clothing / which I put on quickly / at 2:30 a.m. / over my enormous hard-on."[33] The flesh beckoned; it wanted more than the company of silent monks. The mind, too, reeled—all that meditation hadn't freed Cohen of his acute depression, an affliction with which he had wrestled all his life. The only thing that could satisfy both, he knew, was work.

And with that, after an awkward good-bye to Roshi, it was back to Los Angeles, and back to the studio. In his absence, his record label had released a best-of compilation and hoped, like many of Cohen's fans, that when he finally stepped back into civilization, he'd do so with an album to match *The Future* in daring and tone. But everything about the new album—starting with its humble name, *Ten New Songs*—was subdued. Released in October 2001, the album's cover features a blurry photograph, taken by Cohen on his computer's webcam, of him and Sharon Robinson, one of his former backup singers who had become a friend and who cowrote and produced all of the album's songs. Cohen wasn't eager to take credit or reassert himself; collaboration, perhaps, was what one gravitated toward after years of training to overcome one's ego. Unlike its predecessor, the new album offered no anthems and no answers. Neither did Cohen; when a reporter called to ask him how he felt about the terrorist attacks of September 11, 2001, he replied that "in the Jewish tradition, one is cautioned against trying to comfort the comfortless in the midst of their bereavement."[34] It was meant as a spiritual and political statement, but it applied as an artistic one as well—Cohen had little comfort to give. The best he could muster were hesitant sentiments like "I fought against the bottle, / But I had to do it drunk / Took my diamond to the pawnshop / But that don't make it junk." The album was dedicated to Roshi, and was every bit a failed disciple's tentative tribute, beautiful and haunted by uncertainty and the fading sting of defeat. The album sold strongly in Europe and in Canada, but in America, Cohen seemed to be retreating quietly to the position he had held before his brief spell in the limelight—that of a connoisseur's choice, writer of fine and obscure songs. Whatever chance the ten new songs had of breaking out of their anonymity was quashed when their creator refused to tour. He wasn't ready, he said, and doubted if he could still fill seats.

Instead he worked, and immersed himself in a new romance with his longtime backup singer, the Honolulu-born Anjani Thomas. In 2004, just a few weeks after his seventieth birthday, Cohen surprised his fans by releasing another album, *Dear Heather*, an uncharacteristically speedy production for an artist who worked at a glacial pace. He had wanted to call it *Old Ideas*, but was concerned that it would come across as another greatest-hits compilation. Still, much about the album was unmistakably old. It included a cover of Cohen's beloved "Tennessee Waltz," the song he'd grown up listening to Patti Page croon on the radio; as well as a reading of "To a Teacher," the poem Cohen had written to A. M. Klein and that appeared in his very first collection of poetry, *Let Us Compare Mythologies*, in 1961; another reading—underscored by brushes on a snare drum—of F. R. Scott's "Villanelle for Our Time," and a song based on *Un Canadien Errant,* a Québécois folk song. Despite the occasional musical experimentation—vocal tracks doubling on themselves, or a few passages of free jazz—the album felt like what Henry James called "the rest that precedes the great rest,"[35] the kind of equilibrium one achieves only when all aspirations are abandoned and all desires quelled.

The quietude pleased: *Dear Heather* was Cohen's highest-charting album since 1969. "I know it's hard to get a grip on, kids," wrote Robert Christgau, "but people keep getting older. They don't just reach some inconceivable benchmark—50 or, God, 60—and stop, Old in some absolute sense. The bones, the joints, the genitals, the juices, the delivery systems, and eventually the mind continue to break down, at an unpredictable pace in unpredictable ways. Leonard Cohen has had No Voice since he began recording at 33. But he has more No Voice today, at 70, than he did on *Ten New Songs*, at 67—the tenderness in his husky whisper of 2001, tenderness the way steak is tender, has dried up in his whispered husk of 2004, rendering his traditional dependence on the female backups who love him more grotesque." He meant it in a nice way. Cohen's "diminished inspiration" was only normal for a man his age, Christgau seemed to imply, and it was inspiration enough that he was singing at all. He gave the album a B, but not before distancing himself from the singer and his vision. "Not only do I like the guy, I'm Old enough to identify with him," Christgau concluded. "But I doubt I'll ever be Old enough to identify with this."[36] Still, it was a more dignified pursuit than those of many of his contemporaries, and, lacking the burdens of a tour, a perfectly fine and intimate album with which to begin and conclude a rich and strange career. To most of Cohen's followers *Dear Heather* was the sound of things to come; if more albums were forthcoming, surely they would sound like this, a series of sweet and increasingly soft farewells.

And then came the avalanche.

It began with a cryptic visit to the Los Angeles store of Cohen's daughter, Lorca. A man came in and said he was dating an employee of Kelley Lynch, Leonard Cohen's manager. He told Lorca that her father ought to take a look at his accounts. She alerted her father, who rushed to his bank and was surprised to learn that Lynch, a onetime lover and a longtime close friend, had stolen most of his money. It was impossible to say how much of it was gone, but the outcome looked grim.

With the help of a lawyer—Anjani's former husband, Robert

Kory—Cohen began an investigation into his affairs, and each discovery bruised him more. Lynch hadn't just stolen between ten and thirteen million dollars, but had left him liable for hefty tax bills as well. Worst, she had forged documents and sold the rights to many of his songs. Kory reached out to Lynch, but she refused to compromise. In August 2005 came the lawsuits; soon thereafter the harassment began.

After he severed their seventeen-year professional engagement the year before, Cohen later testified in court, Lynch started calling him frantically, sometimes twenty or thirty times a day. She would leave ten-minute messages on his answering machine, mumbling about the Aryan Nation and saying that he "needed to be taken down and shot."[37] She also took to the Internet, where she wrote long posts that saw conspiracy theories everywhere and, at some point, even tried to connect Cohen with Phil Spector's trial for the 2003 murder of the actress Lana Clarkson. On April 18, 2012, Lynch, wearing a blue jumpsuit and cuffed to her chair, was sentenced to eighteen months in jail. She continued to portray her predicament as a "vicious attack"[38] against her by Cohen and others. Cohen, in turn, was gracious. "It gives me no pleasure to see my one-time friend shackled to a chair in a court of law, her considerable gifts bent to the service of darkness, deceit and revenge," he stated in court. "It is my prayer that Ms. Lynch will take refuge in the wisdom of her religion, that a spirit of understanding will convert her heart from hatred to remorse, from anger to kindness, from the deadly intoxication of revenge to the lowly practices of self-reform."[39]

It was a beautiful sentiment, but it left much unresolved. He had some property—a house in Montreal, another in Los

Angeles, and his old place in Hydra—but he was in his seventies and depleted of all of his life savings. The music industry, he knew, had changed; the money was in touring, and he hadn't toured in a decade and a half. Slowly, hesitatingly, uncertain whether or not he'd actually once again step out before an audience, he began to think about the road, collecting band members both veteran and new, rehearsing, arranging, and rearranging songs. A tentative tour, limited at first to small and intimate venues, was booked, beginning on May 11, 2008, in an auditorium in Fredericton, New Brunswick, that seated 709.

When Cohen took the stage, the audience rose to its feet and applauded wildly for two or three minutes, howling and cheering, some crying. In the days before the concert, there was still some speculation, even among ticketholders, that this had all been an unfortunate misunderstanding, that Cohen wasn't really about to break his streak of solitude. But he was really there, in a gray suit and fedora, and if he was moved by the singularity of the moment, he didn't let on.

"This is the first time in 14 years I have stood before you in this position as a performer," he said. Back then, he joked, "I was just a kid of 60 with crazy dreams." He thanked the town for its impeccable hospitality, and expressed his concern for the victims of a recent flooding in the area. Then the band started playing "Dance Me to the End of Love."[40]

It sounded like nothing Leonard Cohen had previously produced. Music had always been his dragon to slay: He had refused its adornments in the late 1960s, had tried to trick it in the late 1980s by abandoning the guitar for the keyboard, and, in *Dear Heather*, tested its tolerance by experimenting freely. There was no sign in Fredericton of the man who, just four years earlier, limited most of his vocals to poetic recitations. On the modest stage, in his first show of the tour, Leonard Cohen sang, his No Voice deep and healed and confident. And he had with him just the band to underscore his newfound vocal courage: From Javier Mas, the aging Spanish master of the *bandurria*, to Neil Larsen, a virtuoso on the Hammond B3 organ, the band, like Cohen, contained musical multitudes, and was sufficiently in command of its craft to play not for Cohen but with him. Introducing each of his musicians several times, Cohen often stepped aside in midsong and allowed for a lengthy instrumental solo. He was no longer the commander of a musical army, lost without his troops. Nearly five decades after he first took the stage with Judy Collins, Leonard Cohen had finally eased into performing. In true Zen fashion, it turned out that all he needed to do to let his songs state their case was nothing but accept Lorca's definition of the *duende* and allow the tightly closed flowers of his spare arrangements to blossom into a thousand petals. For nearly three hours onstage that spring night in Fredericton, he did just that.

"A Manual for Living with Defeat"

The Tel Aviv that Leonard Cohen visited in 2009 was very different from the city where he had clashed with security guards in 1972, or the one in which, a year later, he had accepted a temporary appointment as a member of a wartime troupe of entertainers. It was now a sleek city, modern and metallic, eager to forget that it was rooted in loose desert sand and mired in ancient conflicts. It liked to put on the clothes of its older metropolitan sisters, New York or Berlin, and pretend to be all grown up. But when Cohen arrived, it could no longer play it cool. For reasons ethnic, historic, and artistic, Cohen had always been regarded with a papal sort of devotion in Israel, and his arrival sent Tel Aviv into a tailspin. Demand for concert tickets was so fierce that the phone lines and the servers of the sole ticket office crashed seconds after the sale had begun. Galei Zahal, the army's official and popular radio station, played even more of Cohen's songs than usual, which was a lot; a few days before Cohen's show they broadcast a special retrospective of his work hosted by a star of the country's local version of *American Idol*. Outside the seaside Dan

Hotel, where Cohen stayed, bunches of young men and women huddled in the crisp autumn breeze, hoping for a glimpse of their idol, shrieking whenever a car with darkened windows pulled up. A short distance away, in Rabin Square—the site of the former prime minister's assassination and the most sacred spot in an otherwise proudly secular town—others gathered with guitars, sitting on the concrete, playing and singing "Suzanne" and "Sisters of Mercy" and swaying gently in unison. Wherever you went in town, people asked if you were going to the show. They didn't have to specify which one.

They were hardly alone in their enthusiasm. Everywhere the tour went after its Fredericton debut, it was met by ecstatic crowds. In New York, throngs stood outside the Beacon Theater on an icy afternoon, waiting for hours in the frost for a chance to see their idol rise again. Many of them, bouncing in place to generate some heat and friskily negotiating with ticket scalpers, were too young ever to have seen Cohen play live. They had come to know him through Nick Cave and the Pixies and Bono and the avalanche of Cohen covers that defined much of alt rock in the 1990s. In New Zealand, as in nearly every other place where the tour had touched down, critics wrote of Cohen's appearances as religious gatherings. "The audience sits hushed as immortal paeans, prayers and odes float from the stage," wrote one reporter. "It is hard work having to put this concert into words so I'll just say something I have never said in a review before and will never say again: this was the best show I have ever seen."[1] At the Coachella outdoor music festival in California—one of rock's most exalted gigs—more than one hundred thousand fans were bathed in golden light as Cohen sang "Hallelujah" for more than seven minutes. They were silent as he sang, and howled when he was done. The other acts who took the stage that day were cool, but Cohen was warm; his fans knew that he'd give them more than an easy and passing thrill.

Which is why nearly fifty thousand Israelis rushed to the nation's largest football stadium to see Cohen perform. Outside, kiosks selling replicas of the singer's black fedora did brisk business, amusing Cohen's ultra-Orthodox fans, many of whom wore such hats as part of their everyday religious garb. Special buses coming from Israel's north and south unloaded throngs of fans in the parking lot. In a cordoned-off VIP section nearby, government ministers, generals, bankers, TV stars, and athletes sipped mojitos as they waited for the show to start.

This being Israel, however, the celebration wasn't free of controversy. When he announced that his tour would conclude with a show in Tel Aviv, Cohen approached Amnesty International and asked for its help in setting up the Leonard Cohen Fund for Reconciliation, Tolerance and Peace, through which all of the show's proceeds would be awarded to an organization of bereaved Palestinian and Israeli parents who had lost their children to acts of violence perpetrated by the other side. At first Amnesty complied, and Cohen set up two shows, one in Tel Aviv and the other in the Palestinian capital of Ramallah. It was not to be. "Ramallah," declared the Palestinian Campaign for the Academic and Cultural Boycott of Israel, an umbrella organization of activists dedicated to the isolation of the Jewish state in protest of the West Bank's occupation, "will not receive Cohen as long as he is intent on whitewashing Israel's colonial apartheid regime by performing in Israel." The concert was canceled. Soon thereafter Amnesty succumbed to pressure and withdrew its support as well.

But Cohen was unfazed. He had spent a lifetime resisting the violent currents of politics. He had stared down Maoists and anarchists, people who claimed he was in cahoots with the colonels in Greece, and others who insisted that he was a radical Marxist for visiting Cuba. In life as in music, Cohen was never one for political grandstanding. In one of his favorite passages, an episode from the Bhagavad Gita, the renowned warrior Arjuna faces an army in war and, examining the faces of his opponents, realizes that many of them are his cousins, friends, and teachers. Discouraged, he tells his companion, Lord Krishna, that he doesn't wish to fight anymore and slay his loved ones. "The wise," Krishna replies, "grieve neither for the living nor for the dead." Arjuna, Krishna added, was a warrior, and a warrior had only one duty: war. "You have control over doing your respective duty," Krishna concluded, "but no control or claim over the result. Fear of failure, from being emotionally attached to the fruit of work, is the greatest impediment to success because it robs efficiency by constantly disturbing the equanimity of mind."[2] With peace on his mind, Cohen addressed his fans in Tel Aviv.

"It was a while ago that I first heard of the work of the Bereaved Parents for Peace," he said at one point in the concert, "that there was this coalition of Palestinian and Israeli families who had lost so much in the conflict and whose depth of suffering had compelled them to reach across the border into the houses of the enemy. Into the houses of those, to locate them who had suffered as much as they had, and then to stand with them in aching confraternity, a witness to an understanding that is beyond peace and that is beyond confrontation. So, this is not about forgiving and forgetting, this is not about laying down one's arms in a time of war, this is not even about peace, although, God willing, it could be a beginning. This is about a response to human grief. A radical, unique and holy, holy, holy response to human suffering. Baruch Hashem, thank God, I bow my head in respect to the nobility of this enterprise." There were those who clapped, but for the most part, the audience remained quiet, not in disagreement or in anger but in gratitude for what was shaping into the highest order of communal gathering, a mass of strangers so firmly united by a sense of purpose that silence seemed like the most profound way to assert their bond. Fluorescent green light sticks were passed around, and by the time Cohen played "Anthem" and then took a brief break, all hands were reaching upward, each hand a point of light. Then, among other songs, came "Suzanne" and "Hallelujah," then an encore and a second one. Cohen no longer had any qualms about giving the audience what they wanted. The relationship was different now. He had discovered an intimacy greater than the one he had grasped for as a young artist when he urged the audience to come closer. To bring them closer, he now knew, to be one with his fans, he just had to sing.

And so the third encore of the last show of his first tour in fifteen years began with "I Tried to Leave You," followed by "Hey, That's No Way to Say Goodbye." The humor was well received, but Cohen had one more serious matter on his mind. He lined up with his band as the monks do on Mount Baldy, and recited "Whither Thou Goest," its words taken from the biblical book of Ruth. "Whither thou goest I will go," he solemnly said.

"Whither thou lodgest I will lodge. Thy people *shall be* my people."[3] It was close to midnight now. He raised his hand and parted his fingers down the middle, the ancient blessing of the Kohanim, the priests of the temple. The prophet was coming full circle now. "May the Lord bless you and guard you," he recited, in Hebrew, one of Judaism's oldest benedictions. "May the Lord make His face shed light upon you and be gracious unto you. May the Lord lift up His face unto you and give you peace." And with that, skipping offstage like a man decades younger, he was gone.

This might have been an apt ending to the story: The hero, presumed dead, emerges for one more astonishing act of musical resurrection, having finally learned to master his powers. It was just the story needed in 2008, with the shadow of economic doom still looming large. Cohen, wrote the *Financial Times* with uncharacteristic playfulness, was the cowboy in the white hat, the antithesis to the blustering fools in more expensive suits whose greed and arrogance brought the global marketplace to its knees. "The contrast with the chiefs of then recently fallen investment banks was hard not to notice," read one op-ed. "Suddenly we understood the fedora. It wasn't just a fetching fashion statement from a monk out of his monastery, it was a nod to a different kind of masculinity from the machismo that had got us into this mess. As taken aback by his success as the rest of us, Cohen wasn't trying to be the top dog. Mid-life-crisis proof, he wasn't even trying to be cool. He was just trying to act his age."[4] Cohen, then, was the ideal man for the job of "post-financial crisis elderly sage," an archetype the culture sorely needed. "As if by perfect cosmic alignment," the op-ed concluded, "Cohen descended from Mount Baldy, a destitute poet with the aura of a grandfather, the fame of a proven but not-too-popular rock star, and the mystical promise that perhaps all our pensions might be saved."[5]

Cohen's salvation, however, wasn't just financial; that was the least of it. Having more than recouped his losses in his wildly successful tour, he returned home to Los Angeles and quickly announced another, this time in support of a new album. Released in January 2012, it was titled *Old Ideas*. It climbed to the third spot on Billboard's chart, making it by far Cohen's best-received work in the United States. Like *Dear Heather*, it, too, was "an autumnal album,"[6] dense with the reflections of a seventy-seven-year-old artist who has lived a long and meaningful life and has remained coherent enough to tell about it. But Leonard Cohen was no longer old, no longer timorous, no longer struggling with depression or grasping for drugs or pining for enlightenment of one sort or another. He was thoroughly in the present. Looking within himself now, he saw someone he liked. "I love to speak with Leonard," went the opening verse of "Going Home," the first song on the new album. "He's a sportsman and a shepherd / he's a lazy bastard living in a suit." It continued:

> He wants to write a love song
> An anthem of forgiving
> A manual for living with defeat
> A cry above the suffering
> A sacrifice recovering
> But that isn't what I need him
> To complete.

After decades of refusing to listen, of running wild, of trying just about anything for a shot at salvation, that lazy bastard was finally realizing that his master, Leonard Cohen, was commanding him with a bit of hard-earned wisdom, telling him to stop:

> I want to make him certain
> That he doesn't have a burden
> That he doesn't need a vision
> That he only has permission
> To do my instant bidding
> Which is to say what I have told him
> To repeat.

Permissions

TEXT CREDITS

Excerpts from "The Future," "All There Is to Know About Adolph Eichmann," "On Hearing a Name Long Unspoken," "A Singer Must Die," "Chelsea Hotel," "Sisters of Mercy," "Bird on the Wire," "Story of Isaac," "Avalanche," "Suzanne," "Diamonds in the Mine," "The Wrong Man," "There Is a War," "Field Commander Cohen," "Who by Fire?" "I Tried to Leave You," "Paper-Thin Hotel," "Final Examination," "Blessed Are You," "I Bury My Girlfriend," "If It Be Your Will," "Hallelujah," "Famous Blue Raincoat," "First We Take Manhattan," "The Tower of Song," "Take This Waltz," "Anthem," "Waiting for the Miracle," "The Poems Don't Love Us Anymore." Excerpted from *Stranger Music: Selected Poems and Songs* by Leonard Cohen. Copyright © 1993 by Leonard Cohen. Reprinted by permission of McClelland & Stewart.

Excerpts from "To a Teacher." Excerpted from *The Spice-Box of Earth* by Leonard Cohen. Copyright © 1961 by Leonard Cohen. Reprinted by permission of McClelland & Stewart.

Excerpts from "The New Leader" and "Hitler the Brain-Mole." Excerpted from *Flowers for Hitler* by Leonard Cohen. Copyright

PHOTOGRAPH CREDITS

Frontispiece Leonard Cohen at Isle of Wight: Tony Russell, Redferns.

Chapter One Leonard Cohen blowing smoke rings: © Jim Wigler.

Chapter Two Leonard Cohen at luncheon counter: Roz Kelly, Getty Images.

Chapter Three Leonard Cohen on typewriter: photographer unknown.

Chapter Four Leonard Cohen at Hydra: James Burke, Time & Life Pictures / Getty Images.

Chapter Five Leonard Cohen with pigeons: Gijsbert Hanekroot, Redferns.

Chapter Six Leonard Cohen with cigarette and turntable: Ian Cook, Time & Life Pictures / Getty Images.

Chapter Seven Leonard Cohen with violets: Paul Harris, Getty Images.

Chapter Eight Leonard Cohen at Mount Baldy: © Neal Preston / Corbis.

Chapter Nine Photograph of Leonard Cohen hiding in jacket: Terry O'Neill, Getty Images.

Notes

PREFACE

1 Leonard Cohen to Canadian Broadcasting Corporation, June 12, 1963, Leonard Cohen Archives, University of Toronto Library.

2 The details of Cohen's first meeting with Marianne have slight variations, depending on the telling. His most exhaustive interview on the subject, from which this version is adapted, is with the Norwegian journalist Kari Hesthamar in *So Long, Marianne*, a radio documentary for Norway's NRK radio, September 1, 2005, http://www.leonardcohenfiles.com/marianne2006.html.

3 Bruce Headlam, "Life on Mount Baldy," *Saturday Night*, December 1997, 72.

4 John Lissauer, interview with author, August 25, 2011.

5 British Broadcasting Corporation, "Hallelujah set for chart trinity," December 16, 2008, http://news.bbc.co.uk/2/hi/entertainment/7786171.stm (accessed June 6, 2012).

PRELUDE

1 The Isle of Wight festival was documented extensively by a team of filmmakers led by Murray Lerner. Unless otherwise noted, this chapter is based on Lerner's footage, as well as on my interview with Lerner in June 2010, on Lerner's *Message to Love: The Isle of Wight Festival 1970* (DVD, Sony Music Video, 1997), and on *Leonard Cohen Live at the Isle of Wight* (DVD, Sony Legacy, 2009).

2 Farren had given several accounts of his conversations with Farr, including in this unsourced video interview: https://www.youtube.com/watch?feature=player_embedded&v=6Y22Q9JN0f0#at=231 (accessed July 18, 2013).

3 Ibid.

CHAPTER ONE: "LOOKING FOR THE NOTE"

1 Pamela Andriotakis and Richard Oulahan, "The Face May Not Be Familiar, But the Name Should Be: It's Composer and Cult Hero Leonard Cohen," *People*, January 14, 1980, 53.

2 On the matter of Kafka and Rav Nachman, I owe a debt of gratitude to Rodger Kamenetz and his masterful *Burnt Books: Rabbi Nachman of Bratslav and Franz Kafka* (New York: Nextbook Press, 2010).

3 Leonard Cohen, *The Favorite Game* (New York: Vintage, 2003), 22. "Spitting blood" appears in the manuscript of *Beauty in Close Quarters,* an early draft of *The Favorite Game.* It is quoted in Ira B. Nadel, *Various Positions* (New York: Pantheon Books, 1996), 8.

4 Isa. 11:4.

5 Exod. 19:6.

6 For more on this idea, see Michael Walzer, *Exodus and Revolution* (New York: Basic Books, 1986), 125.

7 George Eliot, *Daniel Deronda* (New York: Modern Library, 2002), 572.

8 Quoted in J. David Bleich, ed., *With Perfect Faith: The Foundations of Jewish Belief* (New York: Ktav, 1983), 289.

9 Nadel, *Various Postitions*, 13.

10 Isa. 57:2–8.

CHAPTER TWO: THE SOUL OF CANADA

1 Susan Lumsden, "Leonard Cohen Wants the Unconditional Leadership of the World," *Winnipeg Free Press Weekend Magazine*, September 12, 1970, 25.

2 Federico García Lorca, "Deep Song," in *In Search of Duende* (New York: New Directions, 2010), 3.

3 Ibid., 12.

4 Ibid., 41.

5 Margaret Atwood, *Survival: A Thematic Guide to Canadian Literature* (Toronto: McClelland & Stewart, 2004), 4–5.

6 Ibid.

7 Northrop Frye, *The Bush Garden* (Toronto: House of Anansi, 1971), 250.

8 Ralph Waldo Emerson, "The Over-Soul," in *The Portable Emerson* (New York: Penguin Books, 1981), 210–11.

9 Irving Layton, "To the Lawyer Handling My Divorce Case," in *The Collected Poems of Irving Layton* (Toronto: McClelland & Stewart, 1971), 15.

10 Leonard Cohen Archives, University of Toronto Library.

11 Michael Ondaatje, *Leonard Cohen* (Toronto: McClelland & Stewart, 1970), 10.

12 Leonard Cohen, "For Wilf and His House," in *Let Us Compare Mythologies* (Toronto: McClelland & Stewart, 2006), 2.

13 Ibid.

14 Ibid., 37–38.

15 Leonard Cohen, "The Sparrows," in ibid., 23.

16 Leonard Cohen, "Saint Jig," unpublished, ms. coll. 122, box 1, Leonard Cohen Archives, University of Toronto Library.

17 Leonard Cohen, "The Juke-Box Heart: Excerpt from a Journal," unpublished, ms. coll. 122, box 1, Leonard Cohen Archives, University of Toronto Library,.

18 Ruth Wisse, interview with author, March 25, 2011.

19 Quoted in *Ladies and Gentlemen, Mr. Leonard Cohen,* directed by Donald Brittain and Don Owen, National Film Board of Canada, 1965 (DVD released in 1999 by Winstar).

20 Ibid.

21 The precise date of this often-quoted appearance is unclear. Most likely it was 1957, the year Sam Gesser filmed his *Six Montreal Poets*, a profile that included Cohen. Snippets from the interview, undated, appear in *Ladies and Gentlemen, Mr. Leonard Cohen*.

CHAPTER THREE: THE PROPHET IN THE LIBRARY

1 Mordecai Richler, *The Street* (Toronto: McLelland & Stewart, 1969), 23.

2 Naim Kattan, "Mordecai Richler," *Canadian Literature* 21 (Summer 1964): 46–51.

3 Leonard Cohen to Esther Cohen, October 7, 1961, Leonard Cohen Archives, University of Toronto Library.

4 Dusty Vineberg, "Cohen Felt Like Punching Richler," *Montreal Star*, undated clipping.

5 Ibid.

6 Ibid.

7 Ibid.

8 Keith Cronshaw, "Let's Be Ourselves Is Poet's Advice,"*Montreal Gazette*, undated clipping.

9 Quoted in Nadel, *Various Positions*, 147.

10 Leonard Cohen, *The Spice-Box of Earth* (Toronto: McLelland & Stewart, 1973), 21.

11 Linda Rozmovits, "A. M. Klein and Modernism" (master's thesis, Department of English, McGill University, Montreal, March 1988), 62.

12 Like all divisions, this one, too, is nowhere near as clear-cut. *Flowers for Hitler*, Cohen's third volume of poetry, was published prior to the December 1964 speech, and *Beautiful Losers*, published the next year, was already largely written. Yet I use the speech here as a convenient point of distinction, and ask that readers forgive this mild stretching of the chronological truth.

13 Leonard Cohen, lecture notes, Leonard Cohen Archives, University of Toronto Library.

14 See Benedict Anderson, *Imagined Communities: Reflections on the Origin and Spread of Nationalism* (New York: Verso, 2006).

CHAPTER FOUR: NOTES FROM A GREEK ISLE

1 Quoted in *Ladies and Gentlemen, Mr. Leonard Cohen.*

2 Ibid.

3 Hesthamar, *So Long, Marianne.*

4 Milton Wilson, "Letters in Canada: 1964 / Poetry," *University of Toronto Quarterly* 34, no. 4 (July 1965): 352–54.

5 Irving Howe, *A Margin of Hope: An Intellectual Autobiography* (New York: Mariner Books, 1984), 271.

6 Mary McCarthy, *Between Friends: The Correspondence of Hannah Arendt and Mary McCarthy* (New York: Houghton Mifflin Harcourt, 1995), 149.

7 Primo Levi, *Survival in Auschwitz* (New York: Simon & Schuster, 1958), 55. Quoted in Cohen, *Flowers for Hitler* (Toronto: McClelland & Stewart, 1964).

8 Cohen, "On Hearing a Name Long Unspoken," in ibid., 25.

9 Cohen, "The New Leader," in ibid., 67.

10 Cohen, "Hitler the Brain-Mole," in ibid., 43.

11 Leonard Cohen to Anne Hébert, Leonard Cohen Archives, University of Toronto Library.

12 The account of Cohen's visit to Havana is taken from Nadel's *Various Positions*, 91–97. Nadel interviewed Cohen about the experience in 1994, and his remains the most comprehensive telling of this period in Cohen's life.

13 Quoted in Nadel, *Various Positions*, 93.

14 Ibid., 94.

15 Ibid.

16 Leonard Cohen to Jack McClelland, Leonard Cohen Archives, University of Toronto Library.

17 Leonard Cohen to Corlies Smith, Leonard Cohen Archives, University of Toronto Library.

18 Leonard Cohen to Esther Cohen, Leonard Cohen Archives, University of Toronto Library.

19 Leonard Cohen to Victor Cohen, Leonard Cohen Archives, University of Toronto Library.

20 Ibid.

21 Leonard Cohen, "The Poems Don't Love Us Anymore," in *Stranger Music* (Toronto: McClelland & Stewart, 1972), 186.

22 Plato, trans. B. Jowett, *The Republic* (New York: Anchor Books, 1989), 288.

23 Eric Havelock, *Preface to Plato* (Cambridge, MA: Belknap Press, 1963), 29.

24 Cohen, *The Favorite Game*, 40.

25 Quoted in Leonard Cohen to Esther Cohen, September 23, 1963, Leonard Cohen Archives, University of Toronto Library.

26 Quoted in the Leonard Cohen Files, http://www.leonardcohenfiles .com/fgame.html (accessed July 18, 2013).

27 Leonard Cohen to Irving Layton, August 17, 1963, Leonard Cohen Archives, University of Toronto Library.

28 Leonard Cohen to Irving Layton, March 29, 1963, Leonard Cohen Archives, University of Toronto Library.

29 Quoted in Leonard Cohen to Esther Cohen, September 17, 1963, Leonard Cohen Archives, University of Toronto Library.

30 Quoted in Allan Greer, *Mohawk Saint: Catherine Tekakwitha and the Jesuits* (New York: Oxford University Press, 2004), 16.

31 Leonard Cohen, *Beautiful Losers* (New York: Vintage, 1993), 27.

32 Quoted in Adrienne Clarkson, interview with Leonard Cohen, *Take 30*, Canadian Broadcasting Corporation, May 23, 1966, http://www .cbc.ca/player/Digital+Archives/CBC+Programs/Television/Take+30/ ID/1742127604/?sort=MostPopular (accessed July 18, 2013).

33 Ibid.

34 Ibid.

35 Robert Fulford, "Leonard Cohen's Nightmare Novel," *Toronto Star*, April 26, 1966, 27.

36 Interview with Clarkson, *Take 30*.

37 Ibid.

CHAPTER FIVE: "ONE BIG DIARY, SET TO GUITAR MUSIC"

1 Quoted in Barbara Amiel, "Leonard Cohen Says That to All the Girls," *Maclean's*, September 18, 1978, 55–58.

2 The account of the party is taken from Sandra Djwa's *The Politics of the Imagination: A Life of F. R. Scott* (Toronto: McClelland & Stewart, 1987), 289–90.

3 For this and other insights into Dylan's connection to Judaism, I am deeply indebted to Seth Rogovoy's *Bob Dylan: Prophet, Mystic, Poet* (New York: Scribner, 2009).

4 Abraham Joshua Heschel, *God in Search of Man: A Philosophy of Judaism* (New York: Farrar, Straus & Giroux, 1976), 185.

5 These quotes are by Sol Litzin, whose book about the *badkhn* Eliakum Zunser Rogovoy cites. See Rogovoy, *Bob Dylan*, 1–2.

6 Quoted in ibid., 30.

7 Vicki Gabereau, *This Won't Hurt a Bit!* (Toronto: HarperCollins Publishers Canada, 1987), 183.

8 Lorca, *In Search of Duende*, 60.

9 Ps. 147:7 (KJV).

10 Jacques Attali, *Noise: The Political Economy of Music* (Minneapolis: University of Minnesota Press, 1985), 4.

11 Quoted in ibid., 29.

12 Quoted in *Ladies and Gentlemen, Mr. Leonard Cohen*.

13 Arthur Miller, "The Chelsea Affect," *Granta* 78 (2002), 237–54.

14 Cited in *Rolling Stone*, "100 Greatest Beatles Songs," http://www.rollingstone.com/music/lists/100-greatest-beatles-songs-20110919/you-wont-see-me-19691231 (accessed August 26, 2012).

15 Bob Spitz, *The Beatles* (New York: Little, Brown, 2005), 587.

16 Ian MacDonald, *Revolution in the Head: The Beatles' Records and the Sixties* (Chicago: Chicago Review Press, 2007), 191.

17 Quoted in Spitz, *The Beatles*, 615.

18 Augustine, *Confessions*, Book 9, trans. R. S. Pine-Coffin (New York: Penguin Books, 1961), 6.

19 Rom. 10:17 (KJV).

20 Deut. 6:4 (KJV).

21 Don E. Saliers, *Music and Theology* (Nashville: Abingdon Press, 2007), 263–69.

22 Jürgen Moltmann, *Theology of Hope* (Minneapolis: Fortress Press, 1993), 105.

23 Quoted in John Walsh, "Leonard Cohen," *Mojo* (September 1994),

http://1heckofaguy.com/2009/06/22/that-leonard-cohen-article-with-his-romanian-girlfriend-michelle-in-the-opening-photo/ (accessed July 18, 2013).

24 Ibid.

25 Ibid.

26 Lou Reed, "The View from the Bandstand," *Aspen* 3 (December 1966): item 3.

27 Quoted in Nadel, *Various Positions*, 146.

28 Interview with John Hammond and Leonard Cohen, BBC, September 20, 1986, http://www.leonardcohenfiles.com/jhammond.html (accessed July 18, 2013).

29 Ibid.

30 The anecdote is recalled in Judy Collins, *Trust Your Heart: An Autobiography* (New York: Houghton Mifflin, 1987), 145–47.

31 Interview with John Hammond and Leonard Cohen, BBC, September 20, 1986.

32 John Simon, in *Leonard Cohen Under Review, 1934–1977* (DVD, Video Music, Inc., 2007).

33 Jarvis Cocker, interview with Leonard Cohen, BBC Radio 6, January 29, 2012, http://leonardcohenfiles.com/jarvis-iv.pdf (accessed July 18, 2013).

34 This summary of Simon's approach is by John Hammond, quoted in William Ruhlmann, "The Stranger Music of Leonard Cohen," *Goldmine*, February 19, 1993, http://www.webheights.net/speakingcohen/gold1.htm (accessed July 18, 2013).

35 Ibid.

36 Ibid.

37 Ibid.

38 Ibid. The phrase is John Hammond's.

39 These are the lyrics as sung onstage in an April 19, 1972, concert in Tel Aviv. A recording—as well as an exposition by Allan Showalter, arguably the greatest living Cohen expert—is at http://1heckofaguy.com/2011/08/01/new-video-chelsea-hotel-1-by-leonard-cohen/ (accessed July 18, 2013).

40 John Simon, interview with author, August 29, 2012.

41 Bob Dylan, "A Hard Rain's A-Gonna Fall," *The Freewheelin' Bob Dylan*, Columbia Records, 1963.

42 Bob Dylan, interview with John Cohen and Happy Traum, *Sing Out!*, October/November 1968, reprinted in Jonathan Cott, ed., *Bob Dylan: The Essential Interviews* (New York: Wenner Books, 2006), 121.

43 Ibid., 114.

44 Quoted in Greil Marcus, *Like a Rolling Stone: Bob Dylan at the Cross-roads* (New York: PublicAffairs, 2006), 70.

45 Quoted in Ian Pearson, "Growing Old Disgracefully," *Saturday Night,* March 1993, 77.

46 Bob Dylan, "I Feel a Change Comin' On," *Together Through Life,* Columbia Records, 2009.

47 Sean Wilentz, *Bob Dylan in America* (New York: Doubleday, 2010), 334.

48 John Simon interview.

49 Ibid.

50 Ibid.

51 Dylan, interview with John Cohen and Traum, 117.

52 Donal Henahan, "Alienated Young Man Creates Some Sad Music," *New York Times*, January 29, 1968, 27.

53 Arthur Schmidt, "Songs of Leonard Cohen," *Rolling Stone*, March 9, 1968, http://www.rollingstone.com/music/albumreviews/songs-19680309 (accessed July 18, 2013).

54 Ibid.

55 William Kloman, "'I've Been on the Outlaw Scene Since 15'; Leonard Cohen," *New York Times*, January 28, 1968, p. D21.

56 Richard Goldstein, "Beautiful Creep," *Village Voice*, December 28, 1967, http://www.webheights.net/speakingcohen/villv67.htm (accessed July 18, 2013).

57 Ibid.

CHAPTER SIX: WAITING FOR THE SUN

1 Quoted in Wilentz, *Bob Dylan in America*, 136.

2 Ibid.

3 The account of Cohen at the Revue and his interaction with Sloman, Dylan, and Mitchell is taken from Larry Sloman, *On the Road with Bob Dylan* (New York: Three Rivers Press, 2002), 352–62.

4 Quoted in Nadel, *Various Positions*, 167.

5 Quoted in Eve Babitz, "Roll Over Elvis: The Second Coming of Jim Morrison," *Esquire*, March 1991, http://forum.johndensmore.com/index.php?showtopic=2340 (accessed July 18, 2013).

6 Ibid.

7 Rom. 8:19.

8 Donald N. Ferguson, *Masterworks of the Orchestral Repertoire* (Minneapolis: University of Minnesota Press, 1954), 60.

9   Leroy Ostransky, *The Anatomy of Jazz* (Seattle: University of Washington Press, 1960), 83, quoted in Jeremy S. Begbie, *Theology, Music and Time* (Cambridge, UK: Cambridge University Press, 2000), 100.

10 Kathleen Marie Higgins, *The Music of Our Lives* (Philadelphia: Temple University Press, 1991), 167, quoted in ibid., 103.

11 Ibid.

12 Manny Farber, *Negative Space: Manny Farber on the Movies* (New York: Da Capo Press, 1998), 135–36. Quoted in Greil Marcus, *The Doors: A Lifetime of Listening to Five Mean Years* (New York: Public Affairs, 2011), 4.

13 Ibid., 4–5.

14 Robert Christgau, *Any Old Way You Choose It: Rock and Other Pop Music, 1967–1973* (New York: Cooper Square Press, 2000), 144.

15 John Perry, *Jimi Hendrix's Electric Ladyland* (New York: Continuum, 2004), 120–21.

16 This imagery is mentioned in Tom DiCillo's documentary about the Doors, *When You're Strange* (Eagle Rock Entertainment, 2010).

17 Quoted in James Riordan and Jerry Prochnicky, *"Break On Through": The Life and Death of Jim Morrison* (New York: William Morrow, 1991), 295–96.

18 Quoted in Nadel, *Various Positions*, 173.

19 Ibid., 174.

20 Harvey Kubernik and Justin Pierce, "Cohen's New Skin," *Melody Maker*, March 1, 1975, http://www.leonardcohenfiles.com/melmak2 .html (accessed July 18, 2013).

21 Quoted in Nadel, *Various Postitions*, 177.

22 Nancy Erlich, "Leonard Cohen," in *Billboard*, August 8, 1970, http:// www.leonardcohenforum.com/viewtopic.php?f=7&t=31973 (accessed July 18, 2013).

23 "Europe's 'Biggest' Fest Set Near Paris Aug. 1–3," *Billboard*, July 25, 1970, 56.

24 Paul Alessandrini, "Antibes, Valbonne, Saint-Paul-de-Vence, Biot ou la longue marche," *Rock & Folk* 44 (September 1970): 60. Quoted in Eric Drott, *Music and the Elusive Revolution: Cultural Politics and Political Culture in France, 1968–1981* (Berkeley: University of California Press, 2011), 191.

25 The quote and the account that follows are taken from Sylvie Simmons, *I'm Your Man: The Life of Leonard Cohen* (New York: Ecco, 2012), 235–39.

26 Steve Turner, "Leonard Cohen: Depressing? Who, me?," *NME*, June 29, 1974, at http://music.yahoo.com/blogs/rocks-backpages/leonard-cohen-depressing-who-me.html (accessed July 18, 2013).

27 Simmons, *I'm Your Man*, 237.

CHAPTER SEVEN: "ALL CLOSE FRIENDS OF THE ARTIST, PLEASE LEAVE"

1 My account of the 1972 tour and—unless otherwise noted—all quotes are taken from Tony Palmer's documentary, *Leonard Cohen: Bird on a Wire*. Palmer was contracted by Cohen's management to record the tour; for various reasons, the film was never widely released. It was finally issued as a DVD by MVD Visual in 2010.

2 Quoted in David Weigel, "Prog Spring," in *Slate*, August 14, 2012, http://www.slate.com/articles/arts/prog_spring/features/2012/prog_rock/the_rise_of_prog_king_crimson_keith_emerson_and_the_futurist_sounds_of_the_1970s.html (accessed July 18, 2013).

3 Quoted in Weigel, "Prog Spring." *Slate*, August 15, 2012, http://www.slate.com/articles/arts/prog_spring/features/2012/prog_rock/prog_comes_alive_emerson_lake_palmer_at_madison_square_garden_1973_promo_ill_cast_comedy_for_fools_the_birth_of_prog.html (accessed July 18, 2013).

4 Keith Emerson, *Pictures of an Exhibitionist* (London: John Blake, 2004), 119.

5 Ian Palmer, "They Won't Bach Around the Clock," *New York Times*, December 16, 1973, 17.

6 Ibid.

7 Weigel, "Prog Spring."

CHAPTER EIGHT: "THERE IS A WAR"

1 The account that follows is based mostly on Mati Caspi's recollections, published on his Web site: http://www.matticaspi.co.il/collaborations/jeneva.shtml (accessed July 18, 2013).

2 Quoted in the now-defunct Israeli entertainment magazine *Lahiton*, November 1973.

3 Robin Pike, "September 15th 1974," *ZigZag*, October 1974, http://www.webheights.net/speakingcohen/zigzag.htm (accessed July 18, 2013).

4 Harry Raskay, *The Song of Leonard Cohen: Portrait of a Poet, a Friendship and a Film* (Oakville, ON: Mosaic Press, 2001), 91–92.

5 Lissauer interview. Lissauer's other quotes are also from this interview.

6   In *Field Commander Cohen*, the album recording of Cohen's 1979 tour, he riffs on the allusion even further, breaking into a few lines of "Rum and Coca-Cola."

7   Talmud, Tractate Bava Metzia, 59b.

8   Quoted in Stina Lundberg, "I Failed as a Monk, Thank God," http://www.webheights.net/speakingcohen/sl2001.htm. (accessed July 18, 2013).

9   The account is taken from Simmons, *I'm Your Man*, 296–97.

10 Quoted in Gabereau, *This Won't Hurt a Bit!*, 183.

11 Simmons, *I'm Your Man*, 299.

12 Kevin Howlett, *Leonard Cohen: Tower of Song*, BBC Radio 6, August 7, 1994, http://www.webheights.net/speakingcohen/bbctrans.htm (accessed July 18, 2013).

13 Ibid.

14 Mick Brown, *Tearing Down the Wall of Sound: The Rise and Fall of Phil Spector* (New York: Knopf, 2007), 303.

15 Introduction to "Memories," concert in Tel Aviv, November 24, 1980, http://www.leonardcohen-prologues.com/ (accessed July 18, 2013).

16 Carl Gustav Jung, *The Collected Works of C. G. Jung: The Practice of Psychotherapy* (New York: Pantheon Books, 1977), 208.

17 Curtis D. Smith, *Jung's Quest for Wholeness: A Religious and Historical Perspective* (Albany: State University of New York Press, 1990), 107.

18 Leonard Cohen, "Final Examination," in *Death of a Lady's Man* (Toronto: McClelland & Stewart, 1978), 212.

19 Quoted in Andriotakis and Oulahan, "The Face May Not Be Familiar."

20 Ibid.

21 Ibid.

22 Brian D. Johnson, "Life of a Lady's Man," *Maclean's*, December 7, 1992, 64.

23 Leonard Cohen, "Blessed Are You," in *Book of Mercy* (Toronto: McClelland & Stewart, 1984), 9.

24 The Smiths, "The Queen Is Dead," *The Queen Is Dead*, Rough Trade, 1986.

25 John Milton, *Paradise Lost* (New York: W. W. Norton, 1993), 191.

26 Ralph Blumenthal, "A Very Old Zen Master and His Art of Tough Love," *New York Times*, December 9, 2007, http://www.nytimes.com/2007/12/09/us/09zen.html?pagewanted=all (accessed July 18, 2013).

27 Quoted in Nadel, *Various Positions*, 232.

28 Quoted in Pearson, "Growing Old Disgracefully."

29 Ralph Blumenthal, "Excerpts from Interview with Kyozan Joshu Sasaki Roshi," *New York Times*, December 9, 2007, http://www.nytimes.com/2007/12/09/us/09zentext.html?ref=us (accessed July 18, 2013).

30 Quoted in Headlam, "Life on Mount Baldy," 72.

CHAPTER NINE: "A SECRET CHORD"

1 Quoted in Barry Miles, *Paul McCartney: Many Years from Now* (New York: Henry Holt and Company, 1997), 303.

2 Quoted in Wilentz, *Bob Dylan in America*, 325.

3 Quoted in "Q Questionnaire," *Q*, September 1994, 170.

4 T. S. Eliot, "Tradition and the Individual Talent," in Frank Kermode, ed., *Selected Prose of T. S. Eliot* (New York: Mariner, 1975), 43.

5 Lissauer interview.

6 Quoted in Paul Zollo, *Songwriters on Songwriting* (New York: Da Capo Press, 2003), 344.

7 Cited in Artur Jarosinski, "Warsaw 1985," http://www.leonardcohenfiles.com/warsaw-85-2.html (accessed July 18, 2013).

8 Ibid.

9 Quoted in Pearson, "Growing Old Disgracefully," 78.

10 Quoted in *Leonard Cohen: I'm Your Man,* directed by Lian Lunson, Lionsgate Films, 2006.

11 Walt Whitman, "Song of Myself," in *Leaves of Grass,* collected in *Whitman: Poetry and Prose* (New York: Library of America, 1996), 42.

12 Marcus, *The Doors*, 51.

13 *Pump Up the Volume,* directed by Allan Moyle, New Line Cinema, 1990.

14 Quoted in Lunson, *Leonard Cohen: I'm Your Man.*

15 Quoted in Joe Jackson, "Songs of Longing," *Irish Times*, November 3, 1995.

16 I'm indebted to Sarah Gallo for pointing out Bono's complex relationship to "Hallelujah," and for helping me see past my own irrational dislike of U2 in understanding the influence Cohen has had on the band.

17 Cohen expressed his admiration for the writer in a 1995 telephone interview with journalist Joe Jackson, http://1heckofaguy.com/2012/06/24/hear-leonard-cohen-talk-about-james-joyces-influence-bonos-cover-of-hallelujah/ (accessed July 18, 2013). "Breathe," a song

Bono wrote for U2's 2009 album *No Line on the Horizon*, takes place on June 16, Bloomsday.

18 Quoted in Sheldon Teitelbaum, "Leonard Cohen, Pain Free," *Los Angeles Times*, April 5, 1992. http://articles.latimes.com/1992-04-05/magazine/tm-1040_1_leonard-cohen (accessed July 18, 2013).

19 Ibid.

20 The event is recounted in Pearson, "Growing Old Disgracefully," 77.

21 Quoted in Zollo, *Songwriters on Songwriting*, 333.

22 Ibid. Emphasis in original.

23 Roch Parisien, "Tower of Song: The Songs of Leonard Cohen," AllMusic, http://www.allmusic.com/album/tower-of-song-the-songs-of-leonard-cohen-mw0000179432.

24 Quoted in an interview with Barbara Gowdy in Leanna Crouch, ed., *One on One: The Imprint Interviews* (Toronto: Somerville House Publishing, 1994), 17.

25 Ted Ekering, "Naturally Born of Cohen," 1997, http://www.leonardcohenfiles.com/killers.html (accessed July 18, 2013).

26 Quoted in Simmons, *I'm Your Man*, 404.

27 Quoted in Armelle Brusq, *Leonard Cohen: Portrait, Spring 96* (video documentary, produced by Armelle Brusq and Lieurac Productions, released in 1997).

28 Ibid.

29 Quoted in *Leonard Cohen: I'm Your Man*.

30 James Joyce, *A Portrait of the Artist as a Young Man* (New York: Penguin Classics, 1993), 233.

31 Gilles Tordjman, *Les Inrockuptibles* magazine, March 15, 1995, quoted in Simmons, *I'm Your Man*, 407.

32 Agreta Wirberg and Stina Dabrowski, *Stina Möter Leonard Cohen*, Swedish TV documentary, 1997, quoted in Simmons, *I'm Your Man*, 413.

33 Leonard Cohen, "Early Morning at Mt. Baldy," in *Book of Longing* (New York: Ecco, 2006), 21.

34 Frank DiGiacomo, *New York Observer*, October 15, 2001, http://observer.com/2001/10/look-whos-back-at-67-gentle-leonard-cohen/ (accessed July 18, 2013).

35 Henry James, *The Portrait of a Lady* (New York: Penguin Classics, 2003), 61.

36 Robert Christgau, http://www.robertchristgau.com/get_artist.php?name=Leonard+Cohen (accessed July 18, 2013).

37 Hailey Branson-Potts, "Leonard Cohen Testifies in Ex-Business

Manager's Harassment Trial," *Los Angeles Times*, April 7, 2012, http://articles.latimes.com/2012/apr/07/local/la-me-cohen-20120407 (accessed July 18, 2013).

38 Hailey Branson-Potts, "Leonard Cohen's Former Business Manager Jailed for Harassment," *Los Angeles Times*, April 18, 2012, http://articles .latimes.com/2012/apr/18/local/la-me-cohen-20120418 (accessed July 18, 2013).

39 Ibid.

40 David Frank, "He Was Fredericton's Man," *Globe and Mail,* May 13, 2008, http://www.theglobeandmail.com/arts/he-was-frederictons man/article719715/ (accessed July 18, 2013).

EPILOGUE: "A MANUAL FOR LIVING WITH DEFEAT"

1 Simon Sweetman, "Gig Review: Leonard Cohen in Wellington," *Dominion Post*, January 21, 2009, http://www.stuff.co.nz/entertain ment/music/gig-reviews/804015/Gig-review-i-Leonard-Cohen-in-Wellington-i (accessed July 18, 2013).

2 *The Bhagavad-Gita* (Fremont, CA: American Gita Society, 1995), 30.

3 Ruth 1:16 (KJV).

4 Gautam Malkani, "Bow Down Before the Sage from Mt Baldy," *Financial Times*, January 27, 2012, http://www.ft.com/cms/s/0/b9bbf310-47ca-11e1-b646-00144feabdc0.html#axzz2b1tbUaE9 (accessed July 18, 2013).

5 Ibid.

6 The phrase is from Jon Pareles, "Final Reckonings, a Tuneful Fedora and Forgiveness," *New York Times*, January 29, 2012, AR22.

Acknowledgments

I had never intended to write a book about Leonard Cohen. My admiration for him, I thought, was as private as it was immense, a kind of big and shy beast that wouldn't last a moment if dragged out into the light. My first debt of gratitude, then, goes to Jonathan Rosen, who, wisely, knew better, and without whose encouragement and efforts I would never have embarked on this journey.

Once I'd committed myself to think and write about my man, I was blessed, as ever, to have the angels by my side: At W. W. Norton, my editor, Amy Cherry, was brilliant and tough, skillfully and joyfully helping my wildest inclinations settle down and take shape. Her assistant, Anna Mageras, patiently helped shepherd me through the thickets of the production process, for which I am thankful. And Anne Edelstein, my inimitable agent and dear friend, lent me her wisdom and her grace, without which I doubt much would have come of this endeavor.

Kezban Ozcan, whom I only just met but whom I feel I've known and cherished for decades, had shown me more extraordinary kindness than this brief acknowledgment can detail, not the least of which entailed facilitating my access to Cohen's personal papers in the University of Toronto's Thomas Fisher Rare Book Library. There Jennifer Toews, Albert Masters, Natalya Rattan, and the rest of the staff proved to be invaluable sources, making the daunting task of archival research much more manageable. Further thanks are also due the helpful staff of the Jewish Public Library in Montreal; to Sydney Warshaw, who diligently assisted me with archival research; to Zev Moses, tireless custodian of Montreal's Jewish heritage, for guiding me around town and educating me about its rich and intricate past; and to Robert Kory, who kindly helped me navigate the necessary permissions required for this book.

Any attempt at writing is, to a large extent, an exercise in standing on the shoulders of others, and the shelves dedicated to Leonard Cohen, though not nearly as populated as they ought to be, feature a host of talented and astute writers. I am grateful to Ira Nadel, Cohen's pioneering biographer; to Sylvie Simmons, whose meticulous research and exquisite spirit delighted and informed me on the page and on the stage I was fortunate to share with her one evening in Manhattan; and to Allan Showalter, known to us Cohen fanatics as the proprietor of the unsurpassable Web site www.1heckofaguy .com, who took the time to read my manuscript and share with me his encyclopedic knowledge of and uncommon insight into all things Cohen.

More insight yet arrived courtesy of those whose lives intersected with Cohen's and who were generous enough to share their recollections with me. Morton Rosengarten told me stories of a Montreal youth; Ruth Wisse gave a portrait of the artist as a young poet; Murray Lerner shared his recollections and his footage from the Isle of Wight festival; and John Lissauer and John Simon talked of the challenges and pleasures of making Cohen's records. I am indebted to them all.

And as writing this book meant, for long stretches of time, occupying Cohen's life far more fully than I did my own, I am deeply grateful to my friends for their advice, their patience, and their support. Todd Gitlin and Laurel Cook have graciously tolerated more than a few progress reports conveyed a touch too enthusiastically over dinner, and Todd took the time to read several early drafts of the manuscript and scrutinize it with all of his rabbinic might; I am grateful to him for his friendship and his wisdom. Tamar Hermesh deserves my gratitude as well, as do Shira Elhanani and Ori Licht, whose love was kindled by Cohen's words. Alana Newhouse and David Samuels brought their incomparable editorial sensibilities, their brilliance, and their humor to a project often in need of all three; their support, and the support of my friends and colleagues at *Tablet Magazine*, means the world to me. I can think of no other publication that would have indulged my obsession with Leonard Cohen as lovingly as *Tablet*, and am very proud to be of it.

Finally, to Lily and Lisa, my hallelujahs, may I be forever worthy of your love.

Index